CW00586154

BUSINESS COA

For a complete list of Management Books 2000 titles,
visit our web-site on http://www.mb2000.com

BUSINESS COACHING

Chris Farmer

2000

First published in 2006 by Management Books 2000 Ltd
Forge House, Limes Road
Kemble, Cirencester
Gloucestershire, GL7 6AD, UK
Tel: 0044 (0) 1285 771441
Fax: 0044 (0) 1285 771055
E-mail: info@mb2000.com
Web: www.mb2000.com

Printed and bound in Great Britain by 4edge Ltd of Hockley, Essex – www.4edge.co.uk

British Library Cataloguing in Publication Data is available

ISBN 1-85252-512-6

Contents

Introduction

The reasons for this book

I wrote this book because I am a trainer. I present ideas to business people like you, who want to get more out of themselves and others. Usually, I present ideas in the form of seminars; fifteen delegates working through the material over a period of two to nine days.

Delegates tell me that the methods I present make big improvements to their abilities as managers and leaders. Some of them asked me, 'What book did you get these ideas from? I want to buy a copy.'

I said, 'I didn't get these ideas from one book. I got them from reading hundreds of books. I acquire ideas from all of them.'

'Then you should write a book yourself – I would buy it.'

That thought stuck in my mind. It occurred to me that it would be more efficient if I wrote the ideas down in the form of a book. That way I can present the ideas to more people. That would be good business.

Then I was lucky to meet James Alexander, the publisher at Management Books 2000.

James said, 'If you write the book, I will publish it.'

I said. 'Great!'

So that is our story.

What about you?

Why should you invest any time and effort to read this book?

There are four good reasons.

1 If you are in business, you are in the businesses of people.

People are your primary resource. People are your customers, suppliers, financiers and workers. To get the most from your business, you need to get the most from people. This book is about getting the most from people.

2 In business, you cannot force people to do anything.

Why? Because we live in a free market capitalist economy. The key word here is free. Only the army, police, customs and prison service are authorised to use force. You, the business manager coach and counsellor cannot use force. Instead, you have to persuade, teach and inspire people to give more. Many people have not learned to persuade. They try to force their ideas. So they come across as 'too pushy'. This book will improve your ability to persuade.

3 Today's economy requires that people continually learn new skills.

So there has to be somebody who can teach. There will be occasions when you are the teacher or coach. You need to develop and train others to become more informed and skillful. You are a life long mentor and coach. But have you ever learned how to teach? Most people have not thought about the best ways to develop others. This book will help you to coach, train and inspire other people. It is packed with interesting and practical techniques. Are you ready to discover them?

4 Everyone has their ups and downs, their strong and weak points.

It is easy to handle a person when they are feeling strong and working to their strengths.

But what about the opposite? What will you do for the person who is feeling weak, and at their worst? What are you going to do?

Occasionally, your role will be to counsel people through tough times. Have you ever studied the techniques you will need? What are you going to say? How will you turn them around? In this book, you will find some ideas that will be like gold to you.

I have divided this book into four parts.

1 Part one is about the attitude of mind needed to be a good coach and counsellor. We will discuss the ideas of 'continuous improvement' and 'optimism'.

2 Part two is a discussion of the key skills that are the bedrock of

both coaching and counselling. The skills are the themes that appear repeatedly throughout the book. They are the 'must have' abilities if you want to improve your results.

The ideas include the practical skills of language, and listening and it also includes important concepts such as building the self-image.

3 Part three takes the key skills and applied them specifically to counselling. We need to discuss the advantages of counselling method, the nature and tactics of counselling communication and a step by step model.

4 Part four of the book is about coaching. We will cover a definition of coaching, then I want to introduce a concept called 'the success formula'. It will be the basis of our coaching model. We will learn how to give effective feedback, both on target 'positive' and off target 'negative'.

We will finish on the concept of 'change' and how change is the essence of improvement.

Before we get into the material, may I just say my thanks?
- To Lindsey for your support and encouragement.
- To James Alexander for having the patience and trust to publish my thoughts
- To the many previous authors who have taught me through their books.

 You will find this key symbol throughout the book. Each time it appears, it is highlighting a vital principle in the effective practice of coaching and counselling in the business arena. Please take good note of these principles as they act as summaries and reinforcing points for your successful performance as a coach.

So if you are ready, let's plunge in and start.

Section one

The Optimist's Code:
Continuous improvement

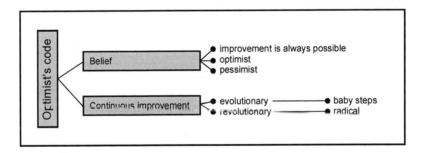

The Optimist's Code

Continuous improvement

All coaches and counsellors have to believe in the principle of 'Continuous improvement'.

Continuous improvement is a belief-system that says, 'No matter what the current situation, improvement is always possible.'

Think about that statement for a moment. Let it sink in.

'No matter what the current situation, improvement is always possible.'

This statement, if accepted as the basis for action, is the root of an optimistic attitude.

Holding this belief as true is very useful for you as a coach or a counsellor. Your role is to help people solve problems and fulfil their potential. So you need to create and sustain the right attitude. If you want to coach people you have to be an optimist at heart.

Imagine you are faced with a person who is in a situation that is causing him or her emotional pain and distress. Imagine you say,

'I know you are in pain right now. But things can and will get better. Let's work out a plan.'

What positive feelings will be inspired in the mind of the other?

Instead of that, imagine you listen to the person's sad story and say,

'I really feel sorry for you. How terrible. You are so unlucky. How does all this make you feel?'

Yes, you are being sympathetic, but would these words be likely to inspire a positive change? Or would they more likely invoke a feeling of sorrow?

A pessimist has an opposite belief to ours. A pessimist believes that, *'no matter what the current situation, it can always get worse.'*

We must never be pessimistic. What would happen if you were in troubled times and you visited a counsellor who was a pessimist? How much help would a pessimistic coach be to you?

Not much.

A belief in continuous improvement, that 'improvement is always possible', will be useful to you both when people are facing good times and bad.

What about when things are going really well?

In those circumstances our 'Improvement is always possible' belief is a guard against complacency.

For example, in 2002, I worked for a while doing some leadership training at a Honda factory.

In the reception of the factory was a brand new example of their latest model. At that time it was a new 'Accord' motorcar, gleaming in the lobby area. I realised its purpose was to demonstrate to visitors the quality of their production. It was presented with a feeling of pride.

I was very impressed with this example of stylish, functional engineering. I even wanted to buy one.

Then, I noticed two Japanese engineers standing in the corner, looking at the Accord. They were holding clipboards and they were making notes.

One of them was frowning. They seemed to be critically analysing their car. They were not admiring it. They were already thinking about what improvements could be made.

I approached them and addressed the nearest man. 'Excuse me. I was admiring your car. I think it is wonderful.'

He said, 'Thank you.'

I said, 'I noticed that you seemed to be unhappy with certain aspects of the car.'

Then the engineer said something important 'You do not seem to understand. We are very happy with the car. But we are never satisfied'.

'Happy, but not satisfied.' I repeated it to myself. That phrase stuck in my mind. It is a key concept.

What if the engineers were 100% happy and 100 % satisfied with their product?

So much so that they produced the same version of the Accord the next year. And then again the year after.

Question   If they kept making exactly the same car, how long would they stay in business?

Answer   Not long.

Create and sustain a firm belief in *'Continuous improvement'*. It creates hope and optimism. It guards against complacency.

So, as a coach and counsellor, remember this phrase:

 'No matter what the current situation, improvement is always possible'.

(Note: we will talk more about optimism in section three)

Two kinds of improvement

Improvement can be and should be continuous. There can be two kind of improvement.

They are:

1. **Evolutionary improvement**
2. **Revolutionary improvement**

Evolutionary improvement
Evolutionary improvement is a form of change that is based upon the principle of making *small daily improvements* to the current situation. Building on what you already have.

Revolutionary improvement
Revolutionary improvement is a form of change that is based upon throwing out the old ways, and *starting from scratch* with new ideas, and new methods.

Let us examine each one in turn:

Evolutionary

Evolutionary change is nature's way of improving things. It is based on the idea that big improvements are the sum total of many small improvements. If a person wants to make big changes in his situation,

12

he can do that by making many small ones. Small changes 'stack up' over time.

For example, I lift weights. If I want to improve my Bench Press by 30 lbs, I start by adding 2lbs to the barbell today.

Over a period of time, my body adapts to the new stressor and I become stronger. When I have adapted to the additional two pounds, I add another two pounds. Slow but steady increases over a period of weeks or months will pay off in big strength gains. If I tried to add on 30lbs of weights all at the same time, I couldn't lift it. I would probably break something – not least, my spirit!

I call this type of progress 'Baby Steps'.

I believe in baby steps because they work. They work because they are do-able. I can see how I can make a small improvement here, a slight advance there. And if I commit myself to continually, (I mean every day), making small improvements, over the year, they stack up to noticeable and substantial gains.

Could you use the same approach to help others?

Could you suggest that the person does not have to create a huge change today, but he could and should make a small improvement. And then another tomorrow. And again the day after. Could you convince someone to engage in a series of small, baby-step improvements?

Yes, you could. Because it is easier to help people make small changes than it is to have them make big changes.

And the good news is that small changes make big changes.

Examples of 'baby step', evolutionary changes are legion:

- car design is evolutionary
- children growing up is evolutionary
- cities developing
- gaining or losing weight
- technological advance.

If positive change is so simple, how come everyone doesn't do it?

The answer is, baby steps improvements are easy to do, but easy not to. Anyone can say, ' *Why bother? Such a small change will not make any difference.* '

And they are right. One small change will not make much difference. So they fail to make the small changes that could contribute to a big improvement.

In fact, through inaction, many people fall into the trap of allowing the principle of 'baby steps' to work against them.

They allow small faults, small regressions, and small degradations to creep into their habits. They say, *'It is only one. One will not make any difference.'*

Many times people find themselves in bad situations because they have fallen behind gradually over years, a little bit at a time. Now they find the numerous small mistakes, taken over months and years have created a crisis.

This could happen in their health, their finances, relationships or business.

You can think of an example of this happening in your own experience can't you? It is everywhere.

So as a coach and counsellor, learn this phrase:

 **'Success comes though baby steps.
Easy to do, but easy not to.'**

Revolutionary

Revolutionary change is the opposite to 'baby steps-evolutionary change'. Revolutionary change is more radical. It is improvement based upon throwing out the old design and starting from new, with a blank slate – new methods, new beliefs and new systems.

Revolutions are dramatic, exciting and costly. They can also be hugely beneficial. Sometimes 'baby steps' is not enough and you will have to coach and counsel someone through revolutionary changes.

For example:

Suppose you were in the vinyl record manufacturing business in the 1980s. You were making the best vinyl records in the country. You were committed to continuous improvement in the form of baby steps. Every week you were thinking of ways to improve the quality and quantity of your vinyl records production.

Then you heard a rumour.

You heard that there was a new music format called Compact Disc, or 'CD.' Apparently, it was possible to record music onto this disc 'digitally' to achieve a far better standard of sound than could be achieved on vinyl records.

But you know nothing about CD technology. You are an expert in vinyl. Your business is not tooled up for CD manufacture. You have millions tied up in vinyl manufacture.

So you say to yourself, 'I am safe. This CD technology will not catch on. Nobody will dump their record collections and buy the same music again on CD. It would be too expensive'.

If that had been your stance, what would happen?

The world is changing. It always has. It always will. As a result, the context in which you find yourself is in a state of flux. It is the same for everyone else too. Technological advances, changes in law, or political culture can make your current methods obsolete.

Sometimes it is a mistake to keep adapting what you have. Sometimes you have to throw out the old, retool, reinvest and start from scratch.

Examples of this type of change are:

- fossil fuel to nuclear energy
- public sector finance to private sector partnership
- Newtonian physics to Einstein relativity
- redecorating the house or selling it
- marriage guidance or divorce
- training and developing an employee, or dismissing and rehiring.

There are huge potential gains to be made with revolutionary change. But with the huge potential gains are the following considerations.

Revolutionary change is:
- usually irreversible
- often expensive
- uncertain in the result
- stressful.

Revolutionary change can be:

- lucrative
- exciting
- liberating
- necessary.

As a coach remember this phrase from the Greek philosopher Heraclitus:

'Everything flows and nothing abides.'

Points to think about

So, as a person who wants to help others through business coaching and counselling, it is important for you to consider some key questions:

Are you committed to being an optimist?
Will you manage your attitude to others and accept the idea that 'no matter what their current situation, improvement is always possible', or will you allow cynicism or pessimism to creep in?

Are you committed to continuous improvement?
Two kinds of improvement: evolutionary and revolutionary. Can you learn to make a judgment? What kind of situation is the person facing?

Is it one where the solution will be found by building on the existing structure?

Or should this person consider a more revolutionary approach?

The answers you have for these questions colour many things, don't they?

Exercise

Grab a pen and do the following.

- Name two real life situations that would require a 'baby steps – evolutionary' approach to find a winning solution.

- Name two situations that would require a revolutionary approach to achieve a profitable solution.

Evolutionary baby steps	Revolutionary - Clean sheet

Section two

Seven Key Principles

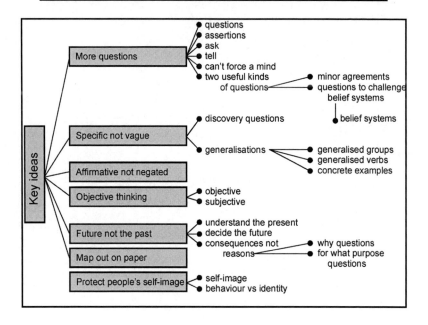

Seven Key Principles

This book has seven fundamental principles that reoccur in different guises throughout. They form the roots of both coaching and counselling skills. We will talk about them in depth, one by one, but let me present them to you briefly here, so you will know what to expect later.

1 Ask more questions, make fewer statements

What happens when you ask people a question? It causes them to think of an answer, either aloud, or mentally. Because asking questions triggers thought, intelligent questioning is the key to influencing others towards the positive change.

2 Be specific, not vague

Some people are not clear enough in thought or language. They have muddled minds; therefore they become unsure and indecisive. If you want to help them, you should train yourself to be more aware of language, and to insist on clarity. Vagueness is a vice.

3 Use the affirmative, not negated language

Affirmative language is talking and thinking about what you do want, would like, and do believe in.
Negated language is talking and thinking about what you do not want, would not like, and do not believe in. Too many people focus their minds on their troubles and the causes. That is, they are stuck in the mental habit of *negation*. But continually thinking about what you do not want is not enough. To help others, learn to have them focus their minds on what they **do** want.

19

4 Objective thinking

Objective thinking is 'the act of identifying the facts of reality without distortion from wish, whim, desire or prejudice.'

If you want to help people, you will want to help them to distinguish fact from fantasy, fact from fears, the objective from the subjective. Many people confuse their 'gut feelings' as proof, their opinions as truth. Your role as a coach is to help them think objectively, and to assist them to separate their facts from their feelings.

5 Focus on the future not the past

The focus of your conversation should be based in the future, not the past. The past is gone. It cannot be changed. The future is not yet here. It can be changed. Your task is to help people to make decisions today that will shape a better future.

6 Map out their ideas on paper

When you are listening to people, you cannot remember everything unless you make written notes. And one of the best ways to make written notes is to learn the mind-mapping technique. When you mind-map what you are hearing from others, it improves listening, stimulates the next question and proves to the speaker that you mean business.

7 Protect the self-image

The self-image is the idea that a person has of him- or herself. People tend to act in accordance with their self-image. If people have a bad self-image, they tend to be non productive. People with a good self-image are usually more productive. So to get the most out of people, always work to build up their self-image. Conversely never attack the self-image.

Key Principle 1

Ask More Questions, Make Fewer Statements

If you were to discover that there was one verbal skill that would dramatically improve your ability to coach and counsel others more effectively, would you be willing to practice it until you were an expert?

That one vital skill is asking intelligent questions.

What is the difference between 'asking a question' and 'telling somebody something'?

Here are some definitions to clarify the difference.

- A question requires an answer in either thought or action.
- A question requires the person to evaluate, or re-evaluate a fact or idea. It causes the person to judge or decide. It causes the person to consider the causes of an event, or its possible implications.
- Questions trigger thought.
- And since human thought directs human action, questions can elicit a change in behaviour.

Let's contrast questions with 'telling':

'Telling' is making an assertion about what you think .

An **assertion** is 'a statement that purports to be true'. So when you make an assertion, it tells me about you, the way you think. That *may* affect the way I act. But it probably won't. I act in accordance to my ideas, not yours. You act in accordance with your ideas, not mine.

So here is the point.

 When coaching and counselling, ask more questions, make fewer assertions.

Some people think that questions are used only to ask for information. But is that the only way you can use them?

No. Questions can be used more creatively than that.

With questions you can:

- ✓ ask for agreement
- ✓ gently challenge a belief
- ✓ gain involvement
- ✓ generate options
- ✓ clarify thinking.

Why is it better to ask questions?

When communicating with others, it is often better to ask questions because people do not like being told.

They do not like being told what to do nor told what to think. Instead, they prefer to be shown an idea or asked to do an action.

For example, which would you prefer: to be told to do something, or to be asked to do it?

Most people prefer to be asked, don't they?

If you are being told what to do or think by someone else, how does that make you feel? Might you feel the other person is being a little too pushy? And as a coach and counsellor you cannot afford to come across as 'pushy'.

If someone keeps pushing you, what do you feel like doing?

Pushing back.

Telling people what you think they should do, rarely works. In fact it is counter productive because 'telling' can set up a resistance in the mind of the listener.

Sir Isaac Newton put it this way,

'For every action there is an equal and opposite reaction'

You are in the business of creating positive changes in others, so you want to avoid doing anything that inspires opposition. And you want to do everything that creates a feeling of mutual agreement.

Remember this fundamental fact of human nature:

You cannot force a mind.

People tend to think what they want to think, not what you think they should think! And as action follows thought, you must influence the thinking of other people if you want to change their actions and improve their results.

You cannot force a mind. It is just human nature. If you try to force a mind, you will lose. So, rather than forcing, why not try leading it, with questions?

Why are questions so much more useful?

They are more useful because they cause the person to think of the answer. The answer may not be verbalised, but it will occur anyway in the privacy of the other's thoughts. And by inviting a change of direction in thinking, we are opening the door on the possibility of new actions and new results.

A second reason that questions are more helpful to you is that they stimulate answers from the inside, as opposed to your attempting to force answers in from the outside. As a result, questions can seem a less 'aggressive' form of influence.

Let me show you an example.

Imagine you are coaching a manager, Julia, who has admonished her colleague, Rebecca, in a highly visible way. You want to help Julia to make changes to her style. Imagine trying this approach using assertions:

> 'Julia. I need to tell you something. I think that you were wrong to speak to Rebecca in front of everyone else. If you speak to Rebecca in front of everyone, you will make her feel angry. So you should take her aside and say it in private.'

The points you make are true and valid, but you are *telling* Julia, so she may fight you.

Instead, what would happen if you asked these questions?

> 'Julia. I noticed that this morning you reprimanded Rebecca in front of all her friends. May I ask you, if you had made an error, what would

you prefer; to be corrected in public, where every one can see, or corrected in private, where nobody else can see?

(Pause)

So, please, next time, Julia, if Rebecca makes another mistake, wouldn't it be better to take her aside and speak to her in private?'

Two useful types of questions

There are two very useful types of questions I would like you to perfect:

- questions that ask for minor agreements
- questions that challenge belief systems.

Let us look at each in turn.

Questions that ask for minor agreements

Being a good coach and counsellor is a skilled job. You need to be able to contradict and challenge others, but in an agreeable way.

You want to avoid unnecessary resistance and conflict. So it is important to ask questions because questions can stimulate 'minor agreements'.

A 'minor agreement' occurs anytime that you say something that causes the other person to say, 'Yes'.

Could you find ways to use questions to stimulate the other person to say 'Yes'?

With every 'Yes' you get, as a coach, you take one step forward.

Questions can have the effect of winning **minor agreements**.

How could you use questions in this way? You do it by taking assertions and transforming them into questions by 'tagging on' a question phrase.

Examples of tag question phrases are:

- ... isn't it?
- ... wasn't it?
- ... can't we?
- ... can't you?
- ... won't you?
- ... won't we?
- ... could they?
- ... wouldn't you?

You get the idea, don't you?

As you speak, gently scatter tag questions, changing your assertions into questions that invite an agreement.

Three things happen if you gently ask for agreements, as you speak.

1. You gain minor yeses.
2. You increase the level of understanding and trust.
3. You 'take them with you', mentally.

Imagine that, as their coach, every time you can win a 'Yes' from the other person, you score ten points.

And your goal is to score points.

If you do not ask for minor agreements, i.e. if you fail to get 'yeses', you may lose. Why?

Because without 'yeses' you'll lose the trust and confidence of the people that you are coaching. If you make too many assertions, they may begin feel that you are not taking their feelings into account.

Another effect of tag questions is they 'hook the mind' of the other person. When you ask a question, what happens in the mind of the listener? He or she answers it.

People do not necessarily answer aloud, but they think of the answer, and that has the effect of keeping them more involved in what you are saying.

Compare that to a person who drones on as they tell you what they think you should do. After two minutes, what happens? You drift off. You don't want them to drift off, so bring them back with questions.

Remember: questions keep people mentally engaged.

Exercise

Look back at the last two pages and count the number of questions I have asked.

Do you think my use of questions was intentional or accidental?

Why do you think I asked so many questions? Write down two reasons:

1 _____

2 _____

Ask questions that gently challenge limiting belief systems

- I define 'belief' as a 'personal evaluation of what is true.'

- A belief system is 'an organised view of the world that affects the person's feelings and actions.'

- A 'limiting belief' is a belief system that puts mental restrictions on the person who hold it. Those restrictions prevent the person from expressing their true potential.

People can only do what they believe they can do. So a persons true potential is expressed only to the degree that he believes in himself. We want to maximise the expression of a person's full potential so we have to maximise that person's self-belief. Putting the same point the other way, we need to have a person break through limiting beliefs.

So, as a coach, your job includes:

- helping people to become conscious of their own beliefs
- helping people to identify contradictory beliefs
- helping people to identify un-realistic beliefs
- helping people to identify dis-empowering beliefs
- helping people to upgrade their self-belief.

All this is done more effectively with questions.

Sometimes, what people *believe* is true, can be more trouble to them than what actually is true!

What I mean by that is, do you know someone who creates stress for himself by reacting to non-existent problems? He responds to events that are in his own mind only.

So as a coach, we may need to challenge dis-empowering belief systems.

Remember – we respond to two things:

1 **reality** (for example, cold temperature may cause us to respond by shivering)
2 **what we *believe* is reality** (for example, an unfounded fear may also cause us to respond by shivering).

26

People are not only influenced by the facts, but also by their beliefs about *what is possible.*

People's 'belief systems' may hinder or help them.

For example, do you know someone who has the education, has the knowledge, but does not achieve what you think they might because they lack self-belief?

You may find that the person you are coaching and counselling either lacks self-belief, or worse, actually holds negative belief systems about him- or herself. The negative self-beliefs hinder their progress.

Under these circumstances, wouldn't it make sense to gently boost people's self-belief, or challenge their negative belief so as to permit them to access more of their potential?

But how? You cannot just say 'Think Positive!' and expect that to work.

Again, the way forward is to ask good questions that will inspire a re-evaluation on the part of the listeners. You want them to re-evaluate and upgrade their own self-belief. Ask them great questions.

For example, imagine you were working with Nigel, who had to make a presentation to a group of important decision makers. Nigel, said, 'I can't make that presentation because I could never stand up in front of all those people']

You could say, *'Don't think so negative. You will be fine. I'm telling you. Just think positive!'*

That would not work, because you are telling, not asking.

Instead, you might ask questions to have Nigel gently turn a corner, like this.

You: The person who can do the best job of this presentation is the person who best knows the material. Out of you and John, who knows the material the best?

Nigel: I do.

You: So are you the best person for the job?

Nigel: Well, yes. But I hate public speaking.

You: Why?

Nigel: It makes me nervous.

You: Is it possible for someone to make a good presentation even though they are nervous?

Nigel:	Yes. I suppose. Provided they knew their stuff.
You:	You know the material the best. And if we gave you the support you needed, do you think it would be possible you could win over your nerves?
Nigel:	I don't know. Maybe it is possible. But I would need you to help me.
You:	When you say help, how do you mean?
Nigel:	I would need help with structuring and organising my material.
You:	If you had that sorted, so you had a step by step plan, would you feel stronger?
Nigel:	Yes. A bit.
You:	So if you and I worked on the notes and built a step by step plan, do you think you could do a decent job?
Nigel:	Yes. I reckon I could.

Great. Well done!

We have gone from *'I can't make that presentation'* to *'Yes I reckon I could'* by asking questions.

 Develop your ability to become a 'skilful questioner'?

Going on. Belief systems may be about other people.

We all have attitudes to 'the world at large'. Some of them are optimistic and some are pessimistic.

Because you want to develop yourself as coach and counsellor, you want to inspire optimistic belief systems in others. That would be a good idea because optimism allows people to access their potential. If people believe they can do something, they will access their creative mind to discover how.

If they do not believe they can do something they will not access their creativity, because to them, it would be a useless waste of time. So optimistic people have a tendency to achieve more – and their achievement inspires even more optimism.

Pessimistic people achieve less. And then their lack of success justifies their pessimism. Some people ask me, 'How can I inspire optimism in a pessimist?'

I tell them that you cannot just say, 'Cheer up. Think positive.

Look on the bright side!' That annoys most people.

Rather, the answer is to continually ask questions that inspire thoughts that will lead to optimism.

Let me give you an example – notice how it is all done with questions. Imagine that Joss starts off.

Joss:	I would like to go for the job, but I would never get it!'
You:	What would you need?
Joss:	What do you mean?
You:	What would you need to get the job?
Joss:	I would need more experience in sales.
You:	If you had that, would you have a good chance?
Joss:	Maybe.
You:	Didn't you have to sell yourself to get the job you are in now?
Joss:	Yes, of course. There were six other candidates!
You:	And weren't you successful then?
Joss:	Yes.
You:	So might you have a chance to get the new job too?
Joss:	Maybe ...
You:	What would be the first thing to do, to get the job?
Joss:	Get an application form.
You:	When shall we get it? Lunchtime?
Joss:	Okay.

Notice that you did not argue. You didn't say, 'Don't be pessimistic. You have to have more faith in yourself' That direct assault on his belief system would fail.

Let us summarise what we have discussed in this section

- Ask more questions, make fewer assertions ...
- ... because, you cannot force a mind.
- Practice asking questions that gain minor agreements.
- Practice asking questions that gently challenge hostile or destructive beliefs systems.

Key Principle 2

Be Specific, Not Vague

Most people are not clear enough in thought or language. They have muddled minds therefore become unsure and indecisive. If you want to help them, you should train yourself to beware of language, and to insist on clarity. Vagueness is a vice.

Discovery questions

To be effective, your coaching and counselling should be based on the facts, not guesses or false information. Commit to being a reality-based, fact-orientated coach and counsellor. As such, you will need to be able to be an expert in the following skills.

I want you to become good at separating:

- fact from imagination
- fact from opinion
- fact from feeling.

It is common for people to become confused and frustrated because they fail at this point.

They believe that:

- the fears they imagine are actually true (without checking)
- their personal opinion has the same status as a fact
- what they 'feel' is true (intuition and gut instinct) is the same as a fact.

So it is important to ask questions that will allow you to discover the truth and separate that from the person's beliefs, interpretations, feelings and opinions.

How do you do this? Ask discovery questions. Discovery questions are questions designed to pinpoint the objective, specific, factual 'evidence' concerning an event, person or thing.

There are three different kinds of discovery questions I would like to discuss with you:

1. generalisations
2. unspecified verb phrases
3. ambiguous phrases.

1. Listen out for generalisations

Making a generalisation is the act of creating a 'universal statement' from the evidence of a limited sample.

We all generalise. It is a form of thinking.

For example, we see that a puppy that wags its tail when it is happy. Then we see another, then a third. We might generalise and say 'All puppies wag their tails when they are happy.'

Now the question arises: is that generalisation true for all happy puppies?

Maybe. Maybe not. Generalising from a limited sample is a natural thing to do. It saves us time and effort, but it not always reliable.

For example, if one policeman treats you harshly, you might generalise and say, *'All coppers are blankards.'* This will be a generalisation based upon one experience.

We often generalise and come to erroneous conclusions, which we then take 'as a fact'. People who fail an exam sometimes say, *'I can't pass exams. Never again!'*

They generalise from one example and react to the generalisation as if it were a fact. Can you see how this might hamper the individual's performance?

 As a coach, it will be necessary for you sometimes to question the generalisations to check that the generalisation is (a) valid reasoning and (b) not outdated.

 First, listen out for any generalised, unspecified groups of people and ask, *'When you say BLANK, who do you mean?'*

Let's go back to an earlier example.

Friend: All coppers are blankards!
You: When you say "all coppers", who do you mean?
Friend: Like the one who stopped me last week for speeding.
You: So not all coppers, but the one who stopped you last week, was a blankard.
Friend: Yes. Him!

Now you have correctly challenged the generalisation and broken the power of the prejudicial thinking, to a certain degree.

Another example.

Joseph: They won't allow it.'
You: When you say "they", who do you mean?'
Joseph: The management.'
You: When you say "the management", who are you talking about?
Joseph: My line manager.
You: So did you really mean "Your line manager will not allow it"?'
Joseph: Yes. Her.

Again, you have correctly challenged the generalisation and made the problem smaller. Now Joseph has to work to change one person's decision, as opposed to fighting the amorphous 'they'.

Can you see that challenging generalisations like these can shrink problems and make them seem more easily tackled?

Here is another example:

Liz: It seems to me there are people who are against change.
You: When you say "people", who do you mean?
Liz: Everyone.
You: Who, specifically?'
Liz: My family for one.
You: Who in your family?
Liz: My dad. He always thinks I am incapable of making my own decisions.
You: So you think your father's against the decision you have made to change your career, is that it?
Liz: Yes.

Can you see again how, by questioning the generalisation, the problem has become (a) more defined and (b) smaller.

The key idea I am making here is this. *Try to get to the specifics.* Do not allow yourself or the other to talk too long in general statements. Get to the individuals, not the general groups.

In addition, it is important you do not to interpret generalised statements in your own way, without checking. Why? Because your interpretation may be different from the other person's meaning.

For example, imagine your colleague, Steve, says to you, *'Nobody gives me the opportunity I need'*

You, the manager/coach might misinterpret this as an implied criticism of yourself. You might interpret this as Steve meaning, *'YOU have not given me the opportunity I need'*

Is that a reliable interpretation?

Suppose you questioned Steve to discover the specific behind the generalisation. The key unspecified group here is 'nobody'. Instead of jumping to conclusions, decide to question the person to discover to whom he is referring.

You might phrase the question as:

You: When you said 'nobody', who do you mean?
Steve: The government.
You: Who do you mean by 'the government'?
Steve: They will not give me the educational grant I applied for.
You: *(persisting with the question)* Who do you mean, 'the Government'?
Steve: The education admissions officer at the further education college in the High Street.

The important things here are:

1. Notice the generalisation.
2. Question and check the generalisation.
3. Be aware that other people often treat their generalisations as facts. Tread carefully.
4. Do not mind-read the other person. Do not assume you know whom he has in mind. Ask him.

What would happen to your effectiveness as a coach/counsellor if you have the habit of interpreting messages in your way, rather than in their way? You would fail as a counsellor wouldn't you? *So ask discovery questions.*

2. Listen out for un-specified actions (or verbs), and ask, 'How do you mean?'

A verb is a word describing an action or a state. Verbs describe what people do, or how they are. Verbs are activities, like reading, writing, understanding or completing. Verbs include 'states of being', like being happy, sad, full, upset, excited.

Many verbs are specific, but many others are vague and generalised. Become more aware of vague and generalised verb phrases. When you hear them, decide to dig a little deeper into the minds of the people you are coaching to have them reveal their exact meaning.

It is important that you do because most verbs have more than one possible interpretation. One way to discover the exact meaning is to listen out for vague or unspecified verb phrases. When you hear a generalised verb phrase, one that could be interpreted in many ways, stop and ask for more detail.

The way to gain more detail about a verb phrase is to ask the question 'How?' or, 'How specifically' or 'In what way do you mean, specifically?'

For example, Michael says, *'I need you to help me with this letter.'*

It might be wrong to say, *'Give it to me then. I'll do it.'*

Why? Because, the verb 'help' has more than one interpretation. The point again is this – find the specific meaning by questions.

You: When you say, 'help', Michael, how do you mean?'

Michael: I mean, do you think I should quote him, word for word, or should I just summarise the meeting?

Discover the specifics. Do not guess at meanings. Do not interpret meanings. Have people clarify their meaning. Ask them to be more specific in their use of language. Language is the tool of thought. So the clearer their language is, the clearer their thinking.

And the clearer their thinking, the better for all concerned.
Another example:

Me:	I am being hampered.
You:	Hampered? How do you mean?
Me:	I cannot find the time to finish this project.
You:	*(checking the verb phrase)* When you say, 'can't find the time', what do you mean?
Me:	I need to prepare my materials for next week's meeting and I need to finish this report.
You:	When you say, 'prepare materials' what do you mean?
Me:	I need to put the boxes in the car ready for Monday morning.
You:	They are already in the car. I saw them this morning.
Me	Oh! Good. Thanks.

Notice how 'being hampered' and 'I don't have time to finish this project' is very far in meaning from 'I need to put the boxes in the car for Monday morning'.

Language is often confused. Do you know people who make things confusing? Your job as a coach is to bring clarity and to impose order on chaos.

You do that by asking for specifics – and one way to do that is asking for specified verbs.

3. Listen for ambiguous phrases and ask for concrete examples

Asking for a 'concrete example' means asking for one of the experiences from which the generalisation was originally drawn.

If you hear vague phrases, it is often useful to ask for a specific example. That has a number of advantages for you, the coach.

- It is an easy question to remember to ask.
- It reconnects the person to reality.
- It gives the person the opportunity to validate the generalisation, or ...
- it exposes the generalisation as potentially faulty or out of date.

Here is an example of 'asking for a specific example' of a generalised phrase.

Elaine: My staff have been making my life difficult lately.

You: How to you mean?

Elaine: They just do not show me the respect I deserve.

You: In what way?

Elaine: In every way.

You: *(Still trying to get an understanding of Elaine's meaning)* Elaine, give me a concrete example of what you are talking about, to illustrate for me what you mean.

Elaine: In the team meeting last week, I asked everyone to be ready to start at nine o'clock and not one of them arrived for the meeting before ten past. The last to arrive did not come in until half past nine. And she never even apologised to me for being late.

In this example, asking for an example is a good way to gain a definite understanding of the vague term 'making my life difficult' and 'not showing respect'.

By the way, I often ask for more than one concrete example. If you can get two or three examples, you will gain greater understanding of the specific factual events that gave rise to the generalisations and judgmental language.

Remember, your task is to get to the facts. Never allow yourself or the other to evade unwanted facts. To move forward, you must help the person identify and understand all the pertinent factors.

How? By asking careful and intelligent 'discovery questions'.

Use Affirmative, Not Negated Language

Affirmative language is talking and thinking about what you *do* want, *would* like, and *do believe in*.

Negated language is talking and thinking about what you do *not* want, would *not* like, and *do not believe in*.

Too many people focus their minds on their troubles and the causes. That is, they are stuck in the mental habit of Negation. Continually thinking about what you do not want is not enough.

To help others, learn to have them focus their minds onto what they do want, that means : Have them use affirmative language.

Affirmative not negated

So, the next two skills to master are:

1. to recognise and distinguish between affirmative and negated statements
2. to ask for more affirmative statements.

Ask people to move away from negated statements and replace them with affirmative statements.

Let me define my terms more exactly:

- ☑ Affirmative statements say what you *want*.
- ☑ Affirmative statements identify what things *are*.
- ☑ They say what you are in *agreement* with.
- ☑ They state what principles you do *stand for*.
- ☑ They describe what you admire, what you strive for, what you think is valuable.

37

- ☒ Negative statement say what you do *not* want.
- ☒ Negated statements say what things are *not*.
- ☒ They say what you *disagree* with.
- ☒ They state what principles you *oppose*.
- ☒ They describe what you *reject*.
- ☒ What things you resist, what you strive against, what you think is worthless.

It is important to have the conversation focused on the affirmative, rather than the negative, i.e.

- what he wants, rather than what he does not want
- what she values, rather than what she rejects
- what they stand for, rather than what they oppose.

For example, at work, many people are clear about what things make them dissatisfied. But, knowing what you do not want is only of limited value. It is not enough on its own, because knowing what dissatisfies, leaves completely un-stated what would satisfy.

Knowing what makes a person unhappy does not necessarily reveal what would make the same person happy. Knowing what career you do not want, does not tell you necessarily what career you do want.

It is not enough to say, *'I don't want X – and here is why.'*

It is more important to say, *'I do want Z, and here is why.'*

Clarity is achieved by knowing what the target is, not what it isn't.

Let me offer you this metaphor. If you were coaching a rifle marksman, what would you ask him to aim at – what he wants to hit, or what he doesn't want to hit?

Obviously, he needs to focus on what he does want to hit.

It is the same for every one else too. People need to focus on what they want. But many people allow the focus to dwell on what they do not want. They focus on their weaknesses; they focus on their fears; they focus on the things that might stop them.

I expect you know somebody who does that.

Who are the people you know, who focus their attention on what cannot be done and why, rather than focusing on what can be done and how?

As a coach, it is important that you learn to redirect their mental focus onto the affirmative. Help them to put their sights on what they want to hit.

You will find that many people have trouble defining the affirmative, but have no problem telling you all about the negative. Your goal is to steer them. How?

First, learn to spot negation when you hear it.

Negation is where someone is trying to explain:

- what he wants by telling you what he does not want
- what he likes by telling you what he does not like
- what he hopes for by telling you want he fears
- what he believes in by telling you what he doubts
- what he stands for by telling you what he is against.

Whenever you hear a negation, ask for the *affirmative.*

If someone says, *'I do not want to do that,'* do **not** ask, *'Why not?'* This will only give you more negative reasons.

Instead ask, *'What do you want to do?'*

If someone says, *'I do not like that idea,'* do **not** ask, *'Why not?'* This will give you the reason for the rejection.

Instead, ask, *'What idea do you think is better?'*

Exercise

In a moment you will read some examples of negated language. Your task is to ask for the affirmative. Practice on the following.

1 'I was against it from the start.' Don't ask, 'Why?' – instead ask:
Q. What were you in favour of?

2 'I cannot do it.' Don't ask, 'Why not?' – instead ask:
Q *(Write your suggestion here)*

3 'I don't think it would be a good move.' Don't ask, 'Why?' – instead ask:
Q

4   'I am against upgrading.' Don't ask, 'Why?' – instead ask:

Q

5   'I don't think we should buy it.' Don't ask, 'Why?' – instead ask:

Q

Remember that we have to deal with reality, and reality is *always something affirmative.*

It is something. There are a trillion things it is not. Talking about what it is not is often fruitless. Talking about what it isn't leaves completely un-stated what we think it is. So negation is only of limited value

Affirmative statements are more useful because they lead to definite action.

When speaking, use the affirmative, not the negated.

Whenever you hear the other person say a negation, notice it and consider asking for the affirmative.

Key Principle 4

Objective Thinking

Objective thinking is 'the act of identifying the facts of reality without distortion from wish, whim, desire or prejudice.'

If you want to help people, you will want to help them to distinguish fact from fantasy, the objective from the subjective. Many people confuse their 'gut feelings' as proof, their opinions as fact. Your role as a coach, is to help them think objectively, and to assist them to separate their facts from their feelings.

Objectivity

As a coach and mentor, it is important to remain as objective as possible with the person you are working with.

It is important to help the other separate fact from feelings, objective reality from subjective emotion. Therefore it is urgent that we discuss the meaning of objective and subjective and learn to use the distinction in thought, language and action.

Here are the definitions you should know. Learn them well.

The objective

The objective refers to facts of reality that exist independent of the person's (or group's) feelings, beliefs, knowledge, wishes, hopes, fears or desires.

- That means that facts are facts, whether we know them or not, like them or not, agree with them or not.
- All our actions, plans and thinking should take place within a context that is in accordance with the objective facts.

41

- If we ignore facts we do not like will we fail.
- If we assume that the things we would like to be true are true, we will fail.
- If we think we can ignore reality and its laws, we will fail.

The subjective

The subjective are personal *evaluations* of the facts, and the *emotions that we feel as a result.*

'The subjective' is our personal world of evaluations, opinions, beliefs, prejudices, fears and feelings. Our emotions flow as a direct consequence of the subjective meaning we ascribe to any given objective event. For example, if someone gives you a diamond ring, it is not the actual ring that makes your heat beat faster, it is the meaning you associate to the gesture.

Remember that many people have the habit of mixing up objective facts and subjective feelings.

For example, a person might say, 'You cannot trust immigrants, (or the Irish, or the Germans, or the French, or Martians or whatever). People take their subjective feelings and confuse them with objective fact.

For instance, Jonathan told me that he felt that his manager, Stephen, was angry with him because Stephen didn't say 'good morning' as usual today. Jonathan assumed that the feeling accurately represented the fact. In reality , the Stephen had been lost in thought and didn't even see Jonathan.

Conversely, people sometimes *evade* certain facts about a person or situation, because it does do not conform to an earlier evaluation. For example, Susan thinks that Joseph is incompetent, and ignores any evidence to the contrary, and focuses exclusively on his occasional errors.

Evasion, by the way, is a common form of subjectivism. Evasion is the act of ignoring, or dismissing a fact, because the evader does not like it, or because it contradicts a long held belief.

An example of evasion would be the husband who sees his wife enjoying a passionate kiss with the milkman, and who then 'pretends it didn't happen'. He forces himself to 'put it out of his mind'. He hopes that if he does confront the fact, it doesn't have to be true. He will not have to deal with it.

Evasion is common. You have probably seen examples. As a coach, one of your jobs is to stop other people evading unpleasant facts. So, can you see that it is a vital skill to separate facts from feelings – objective reality from subjective evaluation?

As coaches, we have to deal with fact and feeling as separate issues, one by one, but remember that all action should be grounded on the 'objective facts of the case'.

Here is an exercise that will help you sharpen your skills in identifying the objective from the subjective.

Read the following sentences, and distinguish the sentences, or parts of the sentences that are objective from those that are subjective.

- That shirt has a brown stain on the front.
- That shirt is a disgrace.

- Steve said that I had sold 20% more than last year.
- I feel that Steve thinks I am really good.

- You idiot. Don't you know how that makes me feel?
- You didn't turn up for our meeting like you promised you would.

- Everything's has gone wrong!
- I have lost my car keys and I have missed my train.

- I don't like the look of him. He looks shifty to me.
- He is wearing white socks and black shoes!

- I know we haven't got the money, but I felt like treating myself.

- We should not give her the job. I've got a feeling she is trouble.

- I know that the deadline is next week, but I am not in the mood to do it now.

Answers

'That shirt has a brown stain on the front,' is an Objective statement of fact. It is a fact verifiable by any observer.

'That shirt is a disgrace,' is a subjective opinion, based on a personal evaluation of what the stained shirt represents.

'Steve said that I had sold 20% more than last year.' is a statement relating to a specific fact, and is therefore more objective.

'I feel that Steve thinks I am really good,' is a statement based upon the speakers feelings, and therefore more subjective.

'You idiot. Don't you know how that makes me feel?' This is full-on subjectivism. It is statement about internal emotions and evaluations.

'You didn't turn up for our meeting like you promised you would,' is a more factual, objective statement.

'I have lost my car keys and I have missed my train,' is a factual statement about the current situation, so it is objective.

'Everything's has gone wrong!' is a subjective evaluation because it is too emotionally charged, and not an accurate assessment of the facts.

'I don't like the look of him. He looks shifty to me.' (subjective)

'He is wearing white socks and black shoes.' (objective)

'I know we haven't got the money, (objective) *'but I felt like treating myself.'* (subjective)

'We should not give her the job. I've got a feeling she is trouble.' (subjective evaluation)

'I know the deadline is next week, but I am not in the mood to do it now.' (objective, then subjective)

How did you do?

Can you pick out the objective, factual identifications from the subjective evaluations and feelings?

If you can, you are learning a vital skill. Most people don't do this. Instead they confuse the two. Confusing fact and feelings causes problems. As a coach, your task is to help people *solve* problems. This distinction will help you to do that.

So why not practice it, until you become an expert?

We know that as coaches, we would do well to distinguish the objective from the subjective. We help the other person to separate facts from their evaluations and feeling.

We base all actions plans on facts. We take subjective feelings into account. They should be carefully scrutinised to make sure that they are based on sound thinking. We know that feelings can be keenly felt but be derived from out-of-date, erroneous, prejudiced or irrational associations. So we must delve into subjective feelings to find their root source. We should check them to make sure they correspond to good sense and to reality.

Let me give you an example of what I mean by separating subjective feelings from objective facts.

In 1997 I found myself working for a company, helping them with selection interviews. We were searching for a new 'trainer and corporate coach' for the business. I was one of four people on the selection panel.

One of my colleagues was a woman called Marie.

We spent the morning interviewing five candidates and in the afternoon, we discussed the relative merits of each. We found ourselves in disagreement over the third candidate, Stephen. Marie didn't like him. She said, *'I don't know, Chris. It is just a feeling. I know he looked good. He had a nice manner, and his CV was strong. But I still have a bad feeling I do not like the vibes he gives me. And I trust my intuition. He is not right, somehow.'*

I knew that there must be some reason for the feeling Marie was experiencing. And I also knew that we should consciously distinguish between the objective and the subjective. So I said, *'Objectively, Stephen is a great candidate. Subjectively, he creates a bad feeling in you. I would like to understand. Please can you explain your feelings?'*

Marie frowned and shook her head.

'I can't put my finger on it, Chris,' she said, *'but he just doesn't feel right. I don't think we should hire him.'*

I said, *'Intuition is important, so please, let us take a short break. During that break, Marie, I want you to introspect. Go inside your thoughts. Discover the source of your negative feelings. We need to know why Stephen feels wrong to you.'*

Marie nodded and said, *'Okay, let me ponder on it. I know there is something.'*

'Then it is important you identify it,' I said.

Marie agreed.

Ten minutes later, I was standing in the kitchen drinking tea and thinking, when Marie burst in. She was smiling.

'I have it! I know what is wrong with Stephen.' She beamed.

'Really? Have you spotted an inconsistency on his CV?' I asked

'No.'

'Have you found out he told us something untrue?'

'No.'

'Have you seen a wanted poster with his face on it?'

'No, nothing like that,' said Marie.

'Then, what is it Marie. What is wrong with Stephen?'

'He looks just like the next-door neighbour I had when I was growing up in Blackheath. And my next-door neighbour once beat me for being in his garden. Stephen looks just like him.'

You can guess the end of the story: Stephen got the job because Marie could separate the objective fact from the subjective feeling.

 Remember to distinguish between the objective and subjective.

Key Principle 5

Focus on the Future, Not the Past

The focus of your conversation should be based on the future, not the past. The past is gone. It cannot be changed. The future is not yet here. It is can be changed. Your task is to help people to make decisions today that will shape a better future.

The future, not the past

You can view time from three perspectives: the past, the present and the future. As a coach and mentor, the most fruitful of these are the present and future. The past is the least fruitful.

Avoid the temptation to delve too much into the past. That is, to discover history. Understanding the past will give you an explanation for the present situation, but it will not necessarily provide you with either a goal or a plan of action.

Understanding the past will give us reasons why things are as they are, but deciding a future purpose sets the direction and gives meaning to the specific goals that will take us forward from this moment.

So as a coach, your task in respect to time is three fold:

1 Understand the present
Discover the current situation both in terms of the facts and the feelings of the person you are working with.

2 Understand the past (in essentials only)
Understand how this situation came into being by asking about the

past events that has led up to this moment, but in essentials only.

3 Decide the future

Ask future-orientated questions. Future-orientated questions amount to this: *'Given the current situation, what is it that you want?'*

- Too many people focus their minds too much on their past – but they cannot change the past.
- Not enough people focus on their present and future – but they can change their present actions, which will change their future results.
- So, from now on train yourself to look forwards into the future and help others to do the same.

As a metaphor, think of it this way:

Jane and Sheena were driving from Bristol towards Central London. They wanted to visit the National Gallery in Trafalgar Square in order to study Leonardo Da Vinci's paintings as part of their college course. Sheena was driving and Jane was reading the map, calling out directions.

After fifty minutes driving, the two friends found themselves sitting in a cul-de-sac on an industrial park in Swindon. They were lost. Both were feeling frustrated and angry.

Sheena turned to Jane and barked, *'How come we have ended up here?'*

Jane replied, *'It's not my fault. You turned left back there.'*

'Yes. Because you said "turn left"!'

'I said, "Don't turn left"!' replied Jane testily.

'Oh, no you didn't.'

'Oh, yes, I did.'

'Well you should speak more clearly. So how come we are five miles from the motorway? Explain that!'

Jane explained step by step how they managed to be on the estate, parked and going nowhere. Jane found ingenious ways to blame the traffic, the map and Sheena's driving. Sheena argued every point and insisted that it was Jane's inability to read maps that was to blame for their current situation.

After twenty minutes of arguing, they finally agreed that it was a mixture of inexperienced map reading, together with unexpected road works and diversions, that were the root causes of their problem.

But now, let me ask you a question – how much use was that knowledge?

The answer is, of course, 'No use!'

How far did the 'explanation of the causes' take them towards Leonardo's paintings?

The whole investigation into the historic causes was fruitless. If you had been there, what would you have advised? Upon what lines should they have based their discussion?

I expect you will agree that Jane and Sheena should have:

- found out exactly where they were
- related that to where they wanted to be (i.e. standing in front of Leonardo's paintings)
- decided exactly what immediate steps they should take to move them towards their goal.

Remember this great truth

People always feel better and are more productive when they are acting to achieve their goals (that are always in the future).

People feel unhappy and are less productive when they feel they are 'pushed about' by events (that are always in the past).

So, *understand* the person's past. But more importantly, have them talk, plan and act with an eye fixed firmly on the future.

Focus on future consequences, not historic reasons

This point follows on from the preceding point.

You can understand a person's behaviour and feelings by relating their current actions to one of two broad categories:

1. the things that have already happened to them
2. the things that they think will happen to them

… i.e. their past or their future.

Likewise, people are **motivated** by the same two categories: Things that have happened to them in the past, or things they expect to happen in the future. People who are motivated by the past relate their current actions to historic reasons.

For example, *'The reason I am not really getting on with my work is because I have been stressed.'* Or

'The reason I am lacking confidence in making the presentation is that, when I was sixteen, my school teacher told me I was terrible public speaker.'

The previous two examples explain current actions and feelings by reference to the past. I call this approach, **living in reaction to events**.

If you listen to other people talking about themselves, most will explain their current actions in terms of the past. They are reacting to what has happened to them.

Not everyone operates in this way however. Human beings are built in such a way that allows them the possibility of projecting their minds forwards in time and creating a vision of the future. It is this 'future vision' that is the cause of their actions. Their actions are decided by their future vision.

They are taking action now because they realise that they live in a world governed by the law of 'cause and effect'. They realise that if they want to create an effect in the future, they must initiate a cause today. They know that the effects of their current behaviour will show up in the future.

These people are acting now, not because of what *has happened* to them, but because of what they *want to happen* in the future as a result of their actions. They may be acting now either to avoid some future problem, or to achieve some future benefit.

To illustrate this point, consider these two examples:

Judith is sorting out her purchase receipts to avoid problems with her tax return next year. So, she is acting **now to avoid a future painful consequence.**

Anthony is eating low fat foods in order to make a weight of 13 stone, so that he can join the Police force. He is acting **now to achieve a future benefit.**

The point here is this – many people you will be coaching are motivated by the past. They explain their actions by referring to historic reasons. But as a coach, it is good to remember that it is more productive for you to orientate others towards their future purpose.

So, always focus the conversation on the long-term consequences of the person's current actions. As opposed to the historic reasons they use to explain their current behaviour.

For example, Ralf was drinking heavily after work. He was drinking two bottles of wine every evening. He had been doing so for over two months. It was beginning to affect him. He was gaining weight, he was losing his mental focus at work, and he was becoming short tempered.

Simon was acting as Ralf's coach. Their conversation went like this:

Simon: You tell me that you are drinking heavily. How much is heavily?

Ralf: Two bottles a night, sometimes more, sometimes less.

Simon: What do you do it for?

Ralf: I do it because I am stressed at work.

Simon: No. I didn't mean 'why are you drinking', I meant to ask – what benefit does drinking wine bring?

Ralf: What are you on about? I am not thinking of benefits. I drink to relax after a tough day at work. Don't you realise the pressure I am under?

Simon: You say you are not thinking of the benefit of wine. What would happen if you did think about the effects? Do you think the effects will be positive or negative?

Ralf: What? Negative I suppose.

Simon: In what way?

Ralf: I have never thought about it.

Simon: *(In a gentle tone)* Think about it now.

Ralf: Well, it makes me foggy-headed and sometimes gives me hangovers.

Simon: Does that add or take away from stress levels?

Ralf: Add to stress I suppose.

Simon: You said you drink to get rid of stress.

Ralf: Well. Short term it seems to help, but long term maybe it may create a problem for me.

Simon: 'Long term it may create a problem.' Do you intend to moderate your alcohol consumption in the next month?

Ralf: I haven't really thought about it.

Simon: Well, why not decide?

Ralf: Okay, I think I should moderate my wine consumption.
Simon: What benefit will you gain if you did moderate?
Ralf: I d be less fuzzy-headed and I'd have fewer hangovers.
Simon: Would that be better for you?
Ralf: Well ... Better of course.

Can you see how Ralf was initially directing his thinking to the historic causes of the drinking, i.e. the stress at work.

Equally can you see how Simon was intent on directing the conversation forwards in time to the future consequences?

When Simon re-focused the conversation on consequences, it triggered Ralf to change his evaluation of his habit from a natural effect of 'stress' to a potential cause of future problems.

As a result of seeing his current drinking behaviour as a potential source of pain, rather than as a strategy to deal with stress, Ralf decided to moderate his habit.

What can we learn from this?
In practice, **do not ask many 'why did it happen?' questions**.

'Why did it happen?' questions give you the history, which is unchangeable and justifies the current actions. As a coach, you may want to change the current actions, so you do not want to have them justified, because that will validate them and make them less easy to change.

Instead, **ask more 'for what purpose?' questions**, or 'what are you likely to achieve if ...?' type questions, or perhaps, 'what is the likely consequence you will create if you ...?' type questions

For example:

Imagine Mike is coaching a manager; Chris. Chris has just shouted at a colleague, Steve, in the middle of a team meeting. Steve had brought the wrong documents to the meeting, which meant that Chris could not give important production figures to the rest of the team.

Steve was embarrassed by being shouted at and said nothing for the rest of the meeting. At the conclusion of the meeting, Steve left without a word to any other member of the team. That was three hours ago and nobody knows where Steve is now. He is not at his desk.

In a quiet moment, Mike decided to give Chris some coaching.

Mike asked him, *'Why did you feel that you had to shout at Stephen in the middle of the team meeting?'*

Chris replied, *'Because I was angry at him for failing to bring the proper papers. That wastes the time of everyone at the meeting. It costs the organisation money and it is not the first time he has done it. I wanted to let him know how strongly I felt about it. He has to be more careful.'*

By asking this 'Why?' question Mike prompted Chris to explain and rationalise, why he was right to shout at Steve. Chris's shouting behaviour makes sense now. In his own mind, it is validated and more likely to occur next time a similar situation arises.

In contrast, imagine Mike had asked these questions of Chris.

Mike: You shouted at Steve in the meeting for bringing the wrong information. What has been the consequence of shouting at Steve in the middle of the meeting?

Chris: Well he got the message that I was not happy with him. He wasted everyone's time.

Mike: I understand that. When a person is shouted at in front of colleagues, what are the likely long-term consequences in terms of that person motivation and confidence?

Chris: Oh, well. Er... He probably feels pretty sore for being told off in front of everyone. But he deserved it!

Mike: If you decided to reprimand people in private, one on one, as opposed to publicly, what benefit would you see?

Chris: They would be less embarrassed and more likely to respond positively to my negative feedback.

Mike: Isn't that what you want?

Chris: Yes. Okay. I get the message. From now on, Ill not reprimand people in public. Thanks for the tip.

So, again the points to remember are:

- Coaching is not done by telling people what you think they should do.
- Instead, coach others with questions.
- Coaching is not done by asking historic 'why' questions, that demand a justification.
- Instead, coach by relating to the future consequences.

Key Principle 6

Map Out People's Ideas on Paper

When you are listening to people, you cannot remember everything unless you make written notes.

And one of the best ways to make written notes is to learn mind-mapping technique. When you mind map what you are hearing from others, it improves listening, stimulates the next question and proves to the speaker you mean business.

Thinking on paper

What happens if you don't record in writing the ideas and thoughts you hear from others? You forget some of them, don't you?

Conversations about complex issues involve many interrelated elements. They may lead to many possible actions. They may invoke conflicting emotions.

As a coach, whose goal is to help someone make sense of his or her situation, it is often useful to 'map out' the conversation on paper.

What happens if you do 'think on paper'?

Neil is an excellent young manager from a publishing company in Oxford. He explains it this way.

'When I map out ideas on paper, I can more easily make sense of what the person is telling me. By that I mean, I can actually see, on paper, how their ideas relate to each other and what the options may be.

I am able to ask intelligent questions to gain greater clarity and accuracy so that I can boil the problem down to a tightly worded phrase or question. That extra clarity is invaluable for me in helping the other person.

As I map out the other person's thoughts, we are both more able to arrange information, evidence, beliefs or fears, and may more easily

54

see any contradictions or flaws in thinking.

So, that means, we are more able to generate possible actions and alternatives together with their likely consequences.

Finally, with all that in place I am more able help the person to make a decision about what to do next. I can more easily move the person forwards, which is the purpose of my intervention as a coach.'

It seems clear that there are definite advantages in thinking on paper, doesn't it?

What happens if you do not map out thoughts on paper?

Nancy is Neil's colleague in the same organisation. She is person who learned the value of 'mapping thoughts' on paper later in her career as a manager. She told me what used happen when she did not 'map it out'.

'I use to coach people by what I call 'active listening'. I listened intently to the person but I found that I was often overwhelmed by too much information.

I cannot remember everything people tell me, nor can I always make the proper connections. So I had to keep checking things I had heard earlier but now was unsure of.

I ended up by listening sympathetically and offering emotional support. Although giving emotional support is nice, I realised I was not assisting the person to identify, organise, evaluate and plan their next move.

So although they came away feeling they had my sympathy and support, they were not coming away from my coaching sessions feeling empowered with a definite plan. I recognised that my abilities as a personal coach were being greatly diminished, simply because I was not taking the necessary effort to map out the conversation and help the person to think on paper.

Since that time I have learned to organise thoughts on paper and as a result I have increased my effectiveness enormously.'

I asked Nancy, *'So, how do you map a conversation?'*

She said, *'The first thing to realise is that you do not have to write a transcript. The goal is to understand the connections and clarify the meaning by drawing flow charts and schematics with lines, arrows and only a few key words and phrases.*

Start in the centre of the page and ask the question 'What is it?', meaning, what is the fundamental issue to be resolved

The more accurately you can identify the subject, questions, issue or problem, the more quickly you will be able to move towards solutions.

Ask questions, generate options, list the facts and the things known or not known. Record them all in essentials only, on the map. Remember that the purpose is to set things up so that you can ask the person at the end of the conversation to make a decision.'

I asked Nancy, *'How did you learn to map conversations so well?'*

She replied, *' I watched how Neil did his and then just practiced at every opportunity – at team meetings, appraisals and interviews. Sometimes I practiced at home by mapping political discussion programmes on the television.'*

I said, *'How long did it take to get to the point when you considered yourself good at this?'*

She said, *'After about a month I was pretty good. You soon get the 'feel' for it and after a while it becomes second nature.'*

'And what difference did it make to you as a coach?' I enquired.

Nancy smiled and said, *'You wouldn't believe it. I would say that I am about three times more effective. What I mean by that is, I actually help people to make definite decisions and take prompt actions. As a result they feel better for having come to me and I count that as success, don't you, Chris?'*

Absolutely!

I said, *'May see some examples of your maps?'*

Nancy said, *'Yes. I will find you some appropriate examples and get permission from the person they relate to.'*

Two hours later Nancy was able to give me a couple of examples and you can see them below.

Look carefully at how they are formed and think about how you might use the same technique to improve your coaching skills.

When you have studied the maps, answer these three questions.

1. How could you get good at this technique?
2. Who could help you by being your guinea pig?

3. What benefits would be able to offer others if you mastered 'mapping thoughts on paper?'

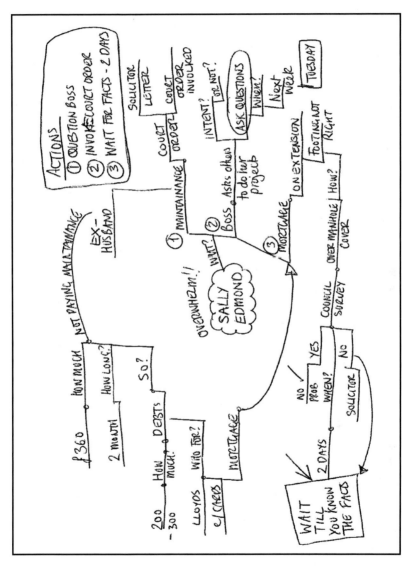

Examples of Nancy's maps

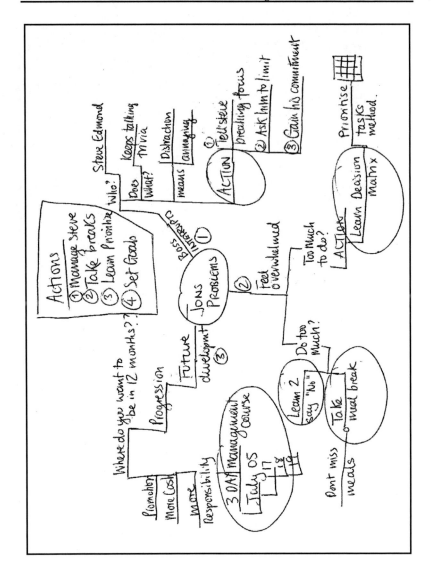

Key Principle 7

Protect the Self-image

The self-image is the idea that a person has of himself. People tend to act in accordance with their self-image. If a person has a bad self-image, they tend to be non productive. People with a good self-image are usually more productive. So to get the most out of people, always work to build up their self-image. Conversely never attack the self-image.

Remember the self-image principle

The 'self-image' is the technical name for something that I know you have heard of,.

- Some people call it the **'ego'**.
- Religion calls it the **'spirit'** or the **'soul'**.
- Psychologists call it the **'self concept'**.
- Sometimes people call it the **'identity'**.

There are many names for it. Whatever you call, it is the same thing. Your self-image is the idea you have about **who you really are**.

My definition:

 Self-image is the mental sum of the thoughts and feelings that people hold about their own abilities and character.

Everyone has an idea about 'who they really are'. At a deep level, we all have a 'personal identity' that we see as independent of any particular action or habit we have. Our behaviours change, but the person 'inside' is constant.

We are more than our actions. We each have a 'soul', an emotional centre point. That 'centre' is the essence of character and it is what I am referring to as the self-image.

As a coach, always remember the Self -image Principle

The Self-image Principle

People act in accordance with their Self-image.

From that one principle, we can derive four very good pieces of advice:

1 Always strive to build up others' self-image.
2 If you cannot build it up, then protect people from a damaged self-image.
3 Never attack or lower another persons self-image.
4 Apply the above three pieces of advice to yourself.

This is important. Spend some time considering the consequences of attacking another person's self-image.

Think about the benefits you would gain if you purposefully and consistently built people up.

Have you ever done something and then later said, 'That was out of character'?

What did you mean? You probably meant, 'That particular action was not consistent with my true nature, the image I have of myself.'

This point goes beyond a person's particular education, class, race, gender or intelligence. It is possible, even common, to see a person who has a good education, bags of talent, and a high intellect, but who fails to achieve his potential because he has a poor self-image.

Then there are other people, like my friend Mark, who lacks a certain education, has many disadvantages, but has a strong and positive sense of self, and is therefore far more productive.

Psychologists have known for a long time that people with a positive self-image are more productive, have better, more fruitful relationships and are more contented.

People with a poor self-image are found to be less productive, have fraught relationships and are less happy.

So, it makes good sense for us, as coaches to become experts at building up the self-image of those around us. People act in accordance with their self-image, so if you ever attack a persons self-image, you will lose ground.

Let me tell you a story that will illustrate this point vividly.

Last week, Geoff from finance, became angry with Richard. Richard had mistakenly deleted some important files from Geoff's laptop.

Geoff cornered Richard in the canteen. *'You lost those files and I needed them! How could you be so stupid?'* he said.

Richard had always lacked self-confidence and self esteem.

Richard's self-image was such that he believed himself to be unintelligent. His father had told him so many times as a child. That belief had buried itself into Richard's subconscious. Every day, the little voice inside Richard's head whispered, 'You are stupid. Try to hide it from the others. They are cleverer than you.' This voice undercut Richard's self-image and his confidence. It took his motivation and it strangled his abilities. So when Geoff called him 'stupid', he had merely confirmed and reinforced Richard's own poor self-image.

When Geoff called Richard stupid, Richard didn't argue because inside, he agreed with the assessment!

As a result, Richard didn't fight, he just sank into an emotion that was a mixture of defeat and depression. His energy levels dropped two notches. His creativity sank and his social confidence buckled. As a result, Richard continued to be less resourceful and less productive.

Imagine what Richard could be if only he had a stronger self-image.

Picture and describe to yourself the effects of a serious blow to the self-image.

 As a coach, never attack a person's self-image. He or she might agree!

Of course, he or she might not agree. What happens then?

Kathryn was half an hour late for a team meeting. This was the third time this month she had been late for appointments. Her manager, Alison, told her that she thought that Kathryn was 'unprofessional'.

This represented an attack on Kathryn's self-image and Kathryn was having none of it!

'Unprofessional?' Kathryn said, red faced. *'I worked four hours unpaid over-time last week. You didn't think I was unprofessional then!'*

An argument followed. Alison said, *'Being on time or early is professional. Being late is unprofessional. You have been late three times this month. So you are unprofessional.'* Alison was pleased with her logic because she could prove that Alison was unprofessional. So she had won the argument. Hands down.

It is interesting to note that Alison thought she won the argument. But let me ask you a question – how much unpaid over time do you think Kathryn has done since that time?

Remember, 95% of the time, people will not agree with an attack on their self-image. Most will fight to protect their self-image. Their pride and self-esteem depends on it.

If you attack another person's self-image based on the evidence of his or her behaviour, nine times out of ten you will trigger a defensive or aggressive response. You will damage your relationship and the person will become less productive.

Always remember

 The best way forward is to build up the self-image, consistent with the facts. If you cannot find the evidence to warrant praise, protect the self-image as you criticise the behaviour.

Let us go back to Alison, the manager who called Kathryn 'unprofessional' and who thought she had 'won' the ensuing argument. Alison's manager is called Stephanie.

Stephanie is an excellent coach and mentor. She understands the importance of the self-image. She was keenly aware of how Alison negatively affected Kathryn's commitment and motivation by coaching her incorrectly.

So, the day after the incident, Stephanie called on Alison to talk to her about the argument she had had with Kathryn. She explained the concept of the 'self-image' to Alison.

Alison looked puzzled; her brow furrowed and after a few moments she said, *'I don't see it. Sometimes I need to criticise behaviour. What am I supposed to do, praise people when they do things wrong? I am all for praise when it is warranted. But I also believe in honest criticism when it is fair and right to give it. Are you saying I shouldn't criticise people?'*

Stephanie said, *'No. You do have to give both critical and affirming feedback to people. Everyone does the wrong thing sometimes. But, as a coach, you must learn be able to verbalise critical messages in such a way as it does not crush the other person's self-image'*

'Yes, but how?'

Stephanie said, *'Remember that you do not have to say everything you think and feel. If you are criticising a person for an aspect of her behaviour, then you probably should not verbalise everything. You can still think and feel anything on the inside. But if those thoughts and feelings are negative, be selective about what you choose to verbalise.'*

'But shouldn't you be honest about how you really feel? That is what my mother always used to say.'

Stephanie said, *'Many people say that. But let me ask you a question – have you ever said things you later regretted, simply because you were angry in that moment?'*

'Of course. Hasn't everyone?'

'Yes. Until they learn to control their language, especially when they intend to criticise. When you are criticising others, you have to be able to, separate 'behaviour' from 'self-identity.'

'What do you mean?'

'Well, let me give you an example. If I said someone was lazy, would that be an objective fact, or my own judgement or opinion based upon facts?'

'Well, I suppose the term 'lazy' is an opinion. If I see you sleeping, I may form the opinion you are lazy. Presumably though, your opinion is based upon facts.'

'Yes. My opinion that the person is lazy is based on my observation. But 'lazy' is an evaluative, rather that factual term isn't it?'

'Yes.'

'And therefore, would it be a "behavioural" or an "identity" statement?'

Alison paused, then said, *'Identity.'*

'Why?'

'Because it says something about the person's manner or general character.'

'And if I criticise a person's character, their identity, what will they be likely to do?'

'Defend themselves, I suppose.'

'How?'

'They might attack you right back!'

'That is right. If you criticise somebody's character, you usually trigger a negative response. Even if you can "prove you are right".'

'So when you said to Kathryn that she was "unprofessional", was that statement a "behavioural statement" or an "identity statement".

'Oh. I see. It was an identity statement.'

'Why?'

'Same reason. Because it said something about Kathryn's character.'

'And what did she do? Did she accept the assault on her character or did she fight right back?'

'She fought back.'

'So, if you were applying the "self-image principle" to this situation, how would you do it?'

Alison said, *'I would not have used the word "unprofessional", nor any other evaluative words.'*

'Then, what other words could you have used?

'Factual words only.'

'How could you have phrased it?'

'I could have – no, should have said something like this. "Kathryn, you are half an hour late for the meeting. This is the third time this month. Please be on time for the next meeting, or at least phone me to let me know you are running late".'

Stephanie said, *'Why would that formulation have been better?'*

Alison answered, *'Because, it was strictly factual without straying into negative identity statements.'*

'Had you said that, do you think you might have had a better outcome?'

'Yes. For sure.'
'Why?'
'Because we could have had a more reasoned discussion.'
'As it was, we both went off the deep end. Now things are worse than they have been for some time.'

Stephanie explained the law of identity to Alison very nicely, didn't she?

Let us summarise.

If you do not like the behaviour:

- do not use the behaviour as evidence to verbalise an attack on the other's identity ...
- not even if you are sure you are right ...
- not even if you are angry ...
- not even if you would feel better for 'getting it off your chest'.
- Instead, always couch criticism in objective, factual language.

Remember that **constructive criticism** is factual, rational, objective and has the effect of preserving the self-concept. **Destructive criticism** is evaluative and emotional. It has the effect of devaluing the self-image and reducing confidence and commitment.

What should you say if you do like the other person's behaviour?

If you do like the other person's behaviour, it is something you want to encourage. Then go ahead. Talk to the other in *subjective* terms. Couch the praise in positive, emotional and evaluative language.

If you do like the behaviour, you can use the behaviour as evidence to verbalise how they make you feel. The praise should be *specific, evaluative and emotive.*

Constructive praise is taking the behaviour and using it as evidence to make evaluative and emotional comments that boost the self-image. Because the praise is based on evidence, the constructive praise strengthens the self-image and has the effect of lifting the spirits and strengthening the relationship.

Here are two examples:

Steve works for an engineering supply company in Loughborough. Last week he made a solo sales presentation to a panel of three directors who were thinking of buying from Steve's employers. As a result of listening to Steve's presentation, the directors decided to place a high value order for Plasma cutters and arc welding equipment.

Joanne, Steve's line manager, was ecstatic when she heard the news. She knew she must praise Steve. She found him at his desk and said:

'Steve, that presentation was excellent. It was well thought out. You had every benefit highlighted, and you pre-empted all their possible objections. I am so pleased with your performance. You did a great job. Thanks.'

Joanne's feedback was factual, evaluative and emotional, just as it should be.

Here is a second example of good, well-crafted positive feedback:

Loren works in an office supply shop, in a busy part of Birmingham. They sell pens, folders, paper, print cartridges and suchlike. The shop has recently had problems with younger people shoplifting. Last Monday afternoon, Loren noticed a group of three teenagers, two girls and a younger boy, hanging around the computer ink cartridges. Loren saw one of the girls put three black ink cartridges into her shoulder bag. Loren breathed a deep breath and approached the gang. She walked right up to the group and said in a loud voice that rang out across the shop floor 'I saw that. Put those cartridges back or I'll call the Police'

The teenagers looked embarrassed at being found out. The girl pulled the cartridges out of her bag and dropped them onto the shop floor. Then the three ran out into the street without saying another word.

Robert was the shop's manager. He soon heard about Loren's challenge, and he was impressed. He told her too. He said:

'Loren, I really respect the way you handled those shoplifters. You put them under tight observation and alerted the rest of the team. There were three offenders and that must have been intimidating to you. But you kept your cool and were professional and assertive. It made me proud to hear how you handled the situation so well.

You are a star!'

Again, this praise was factual, evaluative and emotional, just as it should be.

Here are some examples to help you to practice your 'objectivity' and 'self concept' skills.

Read these examples and give your opinion.

The question I want you to answer in each case is:

Is this effective objective feedback that will protect and build the self-image, or not?

Example 1

Edward made a sales presentation that had missing slides and the wrong customer's name. It said 'Jonstones', not 'Jones and son'

Edward's manager said,

'Edward. That presentation was amateurish. I am disappointed in you because you let yourself and the rest of the team down. For god's sake, you even got their name wrong! Next time be more focused and do your job properly.'

Was that was factual objective, or evaluative and emotional?

What would be the effect on the relationship?

How would you re-word it?

Example 2

Stephen chased another suspected shoplifter out of a store in Chelsea, but the suspect fell and broke his ankle. The suspect is now suing the shop owners for compensation

William, Stephen's manager, said,

'Steve, you acted like a hotheaded idiot! Who do you think you are, Rambo? Now your heroics are going to cost the company money in legal fees and compensation. Next time – think! Just get a description and call the Police.'

How would you judge this?

Write your notes here

How would you judge this?

Compare the above to this:

'Steve. You chased the suspect out of the shop. He slipped over, running from you and injured himself. Now he is suing the company for compensation. Next time, gather evidence with your eyes. Remember every detail so we can build a prosecution case. Do not chase people out of the shop. Instead, call for assistance. I know you acted in good faith. I appreciate your efforts.'

How would you judge this in terms of building relationships whilst giving the critical feedback message?

Section Three

Business Counselling
Skills and Model

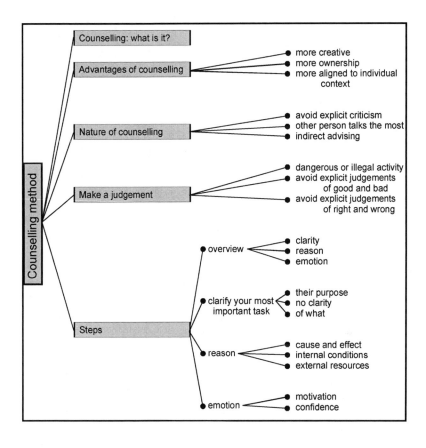

Introduction

Counselling – what is it?

Today's managers and leaders have to inspire and motivate their people though some tough times. That means they need to have good communication skills in general and good counselling skills in particular.

Before we discuss counselling, let us first define it. I define counselling in this way.

 Counselling is a form of non-directive communication, based upon the principle of asking questions to lead people to solutions to their problems, as opposed giving advice or telling people what you think they should do.

Counselling is a specialised and skilled form of communication.

When counselling you are acting to assist the other person to:

✓ clarify his or her thoughts
✓ create new options
✓ make decisions.

Resolve to follow through with action.

Advantages of counselling

What are the advantages of counselling others?

Why not manage people just by telling them what they should do? Because, telling people what they 'should do' is ineffective. Proper counselling technique is often a more effective approach than telling.

There are three reasons for this.

1. Counselling is more creative

Counselling solutions are often more creative. The solutions that come from a well conducted counselling session between two people are better than those that would have occurred had the two tried to solve the problem alone. Counselling solutions come from two minds not one.

- If you are managing people by means of telling, you are attempting to impose your solution on them. That means the ideas are coming from only one person – you.
- When one person is the source of ideas, there are obvious limitations on the creativity, because the ideas come from more limited base. They come from your experience, your knowledge, your interpretation and your imagination.

What happens when there are two minds in the process, instead of one?

- Obviously you broaden the base from which ideas can flow.
- Two people have between them an immense wealth of knowledge, experience and creativity.
- Ideas from one person are the trigger for the second, which may, in turn, stimulate the first. There is a synergy where the creative output of two people is more than twice the creative input of one individual working alone.

So counselling can be a more efficient and effective way of solving problems simply because it depends upon the creative output of more than one person.

2. There is more ownership

Ownership is the feeling of connection, commitment and motivation a person has for an idea or a plan.

Counselling creates a greater sense of ownership than does the 'telling' approach.

If a person is asked to implement an idea or a plan for which he has no sense of ownership, there is little desire, motivation or commitment to see the idea through in practice.

This is not necessarily because the idea is a bad one. Indeed, the idea may be sound and well thought out,. But if the if the person does not feel an *emotional involvement*, or *ownership*, he is less likely to put the idea into practice.

How do you create a feeling of ownership? By involving the person in the thinking and creative process from the start. When people have been involved in a process of creative thought, the fruits of their labour bear their stamp of ownership. The person is much more likely to put the idea into practice with a sense of understanding and commitment.

3. More aligned to the individual's needs and context

If solutions are to be effective, they should be 'aligned' to the person's own context and situation. They should be a reflection of that person's own emotional and personal needs.

If they are not, the solutions will be unworkable.

Now let me ask you a question. Who best knows your context?

Answer – you.

Each person is the world expert on his or her own context. So if you are working to counsel another person, it makes sense to involve the world expert on that person's needs.

A proper counselling approach will have you asking questions that will stimulate other people to contribute ideas and knowledge from their own experience and feelings.

When a solution takes into account all the personal factors of character, emotion and background, it is much more likely to succeed than one that is alien.

The nature of counselling

Let's discuss the nature of counselling and contrast it to normal conversation. In that way, I want you to get a clear idea of what it is you are aiming to achieve.

There are three points I want to make relating to the special nature of business counselling.

1. Avoid explicit criticism
2. The other person should do the lion's share of the talking
3. There should be no direct advice given

Let's discuss these three points separately.

Avoid criticism

As a counsellor, be very wary of criticising another person.

This does not mean that you should 'judge not'. You must make accurate objective judgments of others, their actions and their motivations. It does mean though that you should be careful about verbalising any critical judgments.

As a general principle, assume that people always think that what they do is right, given the circumstances that they find themselves in. If they did not, they would do things differently, wouldn't they?

As a result, many people do not respond well to explicit criticism, even if well intentioned. Your explicit criticism should remain unsaid, i.e. keep it to yourself. Strive to lead the person to a re-evaluation of his or her actions, again by means of careful questioning

Remember this – people are more likely to change their behaviour if they believe it was their own idea to change, not yours.

They change slowly, or not at all if the change is only to comply with another person's expectations.

Here is an example.

Trudy tried for weeks to have her colleague, Stephanie, tidy up her workspace. But nothing Trudy said had as much impact as when young, handsome Daniel, joined the team. Suddenly, Stephanie was bright, smart and better organised. Stephanie changed because she wanted to.

Lead people to critique their own behaviour by offering careful re-evaluative questions.

Here is an example of how criticism went wrong for one Police manager, Inspector McAleer.

Civilian workers often assist regular police officers in large command 'radio rooms'.

Nicky was one such female civilian staff member. She had the unfortunate habit of leaving priority messages 'un-actioned' for too long, in spite of the fact that Police resources were available to be sent.

Last night, it happened again. Nicky took a 999 call from a member of the public who told her that their neighbours were on holiday and they had just seen two youths inside the house. They were in there now, burgling the house!

Nicky delayed sending a police car for twenty minutes, whilst she attended to another task. The original caller phoned again to complain to the inspector, McAleer, about the poor response time. Later, Inspector McAleer took Nicky aside for a 'coaching and counselling' session.

The conversation went like this:

Insp:	Nicky, you failed to respond properly to the 999 call. That is totally unacceptable. Why did you not act and send an officer to the burglary?
Nicky:	Because I had another other call that needed actioning first; I had to arrange for a person to be informed his mother had been found safe and well in Southampton. She had been missing for five hours. She got on the wrong train. She turned up 100 miles away.
Insp:	But that is no excuse. That was a stupid thing to do. The burglary was happening in the moment and needed to be actioned immediately.
Nicky:	Don't call me stupid!
Insp:	Well I am sorry, but it was. You have got to do better next time. If you do not know what you are doing, you can always ask me. I am here to help, you know.
Nicky:	Yes. Right. Is that all?
Insp:	Yes. Thank you for stopping by. Please remember what I said.
Nicky:	Yes, sir.

How well do you think Inspector McAleer did during that session?

At what point, specifically did he mess up? I mean, what was the word that triggered the negative response? I don't know about you, but I think he lost everything when he used the word 'stupid'.

Nicky didn't think she had been stupid. She had a principled reason for her decision. Inspector Mc Aleer never discovered it, and so could not ask Nicky to re-evaluate. When Nicky left the inspector, do you think she was more likely to be thinking about her performance or his performance?

Nicky spent the rest of the shift going over in her mind what McAleer had said, not what she had done. As a result of their conversation, do you think Nicky's level of commitment to the organisation went up, or down? Down of course, because hardly anyone takes criticism with pleasure. Many people fight criticism, even when it is valid.

So we must learn new ways.

Here is an alternative interview with a new Inspector McAleer.

As you read this alternative example, please notice:

1. The use of questions
2. The lack of criticism
3. The attempts to have Nicky re-evaluate her own actions.

Insp: Nicky, yesterday you had two successive calls. The first was a 'Missing person has been found' message to be delivered; the second was a 'burglary in progress' message. Of the two, which one had the greatest urgency? I mean which one most needed to be answered within five minutes?

Nicky: I did the lost person found first because I believe that life is more important than property. The Missing Person Found was about life, and the burglary was about property. In the burglary, no one was in danger, only property.

Insp: I understand life is more important than property. I am not asking about the relative 'value', I am thinking about urgency – time pressure. Which job had the greatest urgency, not value – the greatest urgency, the burglary in progress or the missing person?

Nicky: (pause) I am not sure what you mean.

Insp: Would there have been any great negative impact had the 'missing person found' message been delivered twenty minutes later?

Nicky: Not really, no.

Insp: But what if we are twenty minutes late for a burglary in progress? The burglary was urgent. It had a high degree of time pressure attached to it. I mean, how long do burglars hang around at the scene?

Nicky: Not long. Minutes.

Insp: In the radio room, we must evaluate calls according to two

75

principles 'urgency', deadline pressure, and 'importance', that means 'value'. Urgency and value have to be considered together. Not value divorced from urgency. Do you see the point?

Nicky: I think so, yes?

Insp: What point do you think I am trying to make?

Nicky: That I should consider urgency, as well as importance when I am prioritising tasks; that the burglary had more urgency, even though it was a property crime; that the missing person was important but not urgent. It could have waited. The burglary was urgent and should have been acted on immediately.

Insp: Excellent. Good. If you are unsure on the 'urgency' or 'importance' status of any particular task, you can always ask me. I am here to make those judgments with you. Okay?

Nicky: Sorry. I thought I was doing the right thing, but I see now where you are coming from. Thank you. That is interesting: Urgency and importance … I will think about that. Is that all, Sir?

Insp: Yes. It is.

Nicky: Thanks again sir. Bye

Inspector McAleer handled the interview better the second time, didn't he?

In the second interview:

- ✓ he refrained from all criticism
- ✓ he uncovered the reasoned thinking behind Nicky's error
- ✓ he stimulated her to re-evaluate her method
- ✓ he had Nicky confirm her understanding of the principle of urgency
- ✓ she left, pondering the significance of the distinction between urgency and importance
- ✓ she felt more motivated and involved with her work
- ✓ the relationship between Inspector McAleer and Nicky was strengthened
- ✓ Nicky was more likely to ask for help in the future
- ✓ Nicky is more likely to make more accurate priority decisions

All-round, Inspector McAleer did a good job.

As a management counsellor, avoid verbalising criticism

Let the other person do the lion's share of the talking

What is the balance between speaking and listening in a normal conversation? About fifty-fifty.

That means people share conversations. People alternate between speaking and listening – they let each other speak for a while, before taking the lead. In counselling situations though, the balance between speakers does not have to be fifty-fifty. One person should do most of the talking, the other most of the listening.

In most counselling situations, who do you think should do the majority of the talking? Is it you, the counsellor, or the other person?

The other person, of course.

Why? Because if you are the one doing the talking, you are not counselling, you are advising. And you know what most people think of your of advice. Generally, advice does not cause people to change.

For example, we are all advised to eat less and exercise more, but how many people eat too much and do not exercise? Similarly, we are all advised to save 10% or more of our income towards our retirement, but how many actually do?

As a counsellor, what should be the percentage split between listening and speaking? Would you agree that the other person should be doing most of the talking? If the other person is talking, he is thinking more, and maybe, in the throes of changing.

If you do the talking, the other person is thinking less. He may 'glaze over' and will not be changing.

When you are counselling, do less talking. If you are not talking, what are you doing? You should be doing many things simultaneously, including:

Listening
Paying attention to what the person is saying, and maybe to what she is **avoiding**.

Watching
Looking for the non-verbal clues contained in the person's body language.

Recording
Making written notes as the person is speaking, in order to clarify and understand.

Formulating great questions
As a counsellor, you are asking questions to probe for detail, stimulate thinking, generating options and possible solutions.

Thinking ahead
You are making judgments and evaluations, trying to figure out how you can best support the other person to solve their own problems.

Counselling requires that you advise indirectly
Counselling is not an opportunity for you to tell people what you think they should do. Nor is it an opportunity for you to tell the person what you did when you faced a similar situation.

It is your opportunity to help others to identify the facts facing them, then decide their priorities, organise their plans and inspire their desire to take action.

This does not mean that you cannot or should not advise, but the advice must be indirect. What I mean by that is, you may have definite ideas about what is the correct action to take, but you should lead the person to an answer by asking the right questions. You should not try to push your advice or tell the person what to do.

Here is another example of how NOT to do it.

Rebecca worked in an advertising sales office, prospecting on the telephone for new business. One morning she went to see her manager, Tracy, concerning her problematic working relationship with Joanne, a work colleague who sat next to Rebecca in the office.

The essence of the problem was that Joanne, being older, more experience and more confident, talked to Rebecca as if she were her personal assistant. Joanne insisted that Rebecca made coffee and tea, and ran errands. Yesterday Joanne had Rebecca collecting her faxes from the machine.

Rebecca was a person who 'doesn't like to make a fuss' and so she had been complying with Joanne's instructions, but recently, the situation had been getting worse. Joanne was asking Rebecca to do more, and Rebecca was feeling frustrated, but unable to stand up to Joanne.

We join the conversation at the point when Rebecca has explained the situation and Tracy, the manager/counsellor, is speaking:

Tracy: So, I take it you want me, as your supervisor, to have a quiet word with Joanne. Is that right?

Rebecca: No. Not really. I didn't want you to get involved, as such. I don't want the rest of the team to think I am a tell tale.

Tracy: Then why tell me at all?

Rebecca: Because, I wanted to ask for some advice. What do you think I should do?

Tracy: I'll tell you what you should do. You should tell Joanne straight. Tell her to get lost! If that were me, I would have told where to go, weeks ago! You should learn to stick up for yourself, Rebecca. People take advantage.

Rebecca: I really don't feel I could say that. It isn't really the way I like to go about things.

Tracy: Take it from me, Rebecca, I know people like Joanne. You have to be as firm as they are or they will walk all over you. If she gives you any more trouble, let me know. I will sort the situation out for you. Okay? I hope that helps. Let me know how things turn out.

Rebecca: Oh. Yes. Thank you. I will. Thank you for seeing me.

How did you rate Tracy's counselling skills?

In the space below, write down three things that you think Tracy did wrong, together with what she should have done, instead.

What did Tracy do wrong?	What should Tracy have done?

Tracy should not have imposed her solutions on Rebecca – they did not fit Rebecca's character. Tracy was projecting her character onto Rebecca and expecting it to stick. But Rebecca is not Tracy. So Rebecca has to find a way that will match her own style. It was Tracy's job, as a counsellor to help Rebecca to identify her way forward, that accords to her nature.

So here is an alternative interview. This time, Tracy does things differently. We are picking it up from the same point in time.

Tracy: I understand. You think Joanne treats you like her personal assistant. Is that the essence of the problem?

Rebecca: Yes. I don't know what to do about it. What do you think?

Tracy: What I think you should do is not the issue. How do you want the situation to be between Joanne and yourself?

Rebecca: I want to be just professionally friendly. But she wants me to do as she says, which I do not want to do. I am stuck.

Tracy: So there are two outcomes here – Joanne's outcome, which seems to be ' to control you', and yours, which is for her 'not to control you'. Two opposite motivations, is the source of your conflict. Is that right?

Rebecca: Yes.

Tracy: Whose outcome are you going to let determine your actions, your outcome, or Joanne's?

Rebecca: It should be mine, I suppose.

Tracy: You said, 'I suppose'. Are you unsure?

Rebecca: No. I am sure. I should work towards my outcome. Not Joanne's

Tracy: Why?

Rebecca: Because, her telling me what to do is unfair and shows no respect.

Tracy: So are you saying that you want more fairness from Joanne?

Rebecca: Yes. I suppose I am.

Tracy: How are you going to word it, when you speak to her?

Rebecca: I will tell her she will have to do her own errands and make her own drinks.

Tracy: If you did say that, how would you feel?

Rebecca: Nervous, but glad I did it.

Tracy: If you do not say anything and let things continue as they are, how will you feel?

Rebecca: Terrible. It cannot go on like this.

Tracy: So, tell me again what you are going to do, the next time Joanne tells you to make her coffee?

Rebecca: I will tell her 'no'. The next time, she will have to make her own!

Tracy: So what help did you want from me today?

Rebecca: Oh.. none really. Actually I think I have sorted it. I don't need any help. Thank you, anyway.

As Rebecca leaves, Tracy smiles to herself ...

This time, how do you rate Tracy's counselling skills? Better this time, aren't they?

In the space below, write down three things that you think Tracy did right, together with why it was important.

What did Tracy do right?	Why was it important?

 To summaries this section, remember these three rules.

1. **Avoid criticism.**

2. **Do not talk too much.**

3. **Give no direct advice.**

Making judgements

You know now that, as a counsellor, you will not advise explicitly. But you should keep thinking and judging. As a thinking counsellor, you may have to make the following judgments and act accordingly.

- Judge between legal and illegal actions.
- Judge between dangerous and safe actions.
- Judge between right and wrong actions.
- Judge between good and bad actions.

Here is an example of a manager having to act as a counsellor with respect to a dangerous activity.

Michael is a manger in a company that manufactures seating units for public transport vehicles. One morning an accident occurred involving Adrian. Adrian had been driving a forklift truck and had reversed it into ten stacked wooden pallets. The top two pallets fell off the stack and narrowly missed Rachel, a fellow worker. She was unhurt, but she was shaken by her near-death experience.

Michael asked Adrian to meet him at after lunch for a 'private word' about the incident. At one o clock, Michael met with Adrian.

During their conversation, Michael learned that Adrian had not slept at all the night before, and only three hours the night previously. Consequently Adrian was very tired – his tiredness had probably contributed to the accident.

As you read the counselling interview that Michael had with Adrian, notice two things.

- The manager, Michael, uses questions all the way through this scenario.
- Michael does not get drawn into the reasons, but rather focuses on the solutions to the problem.

This is how the interview went.

Michael: I understand you were tired from having no sleep. When you are driving at work, you need to be mentally and physical capable of the task, don't you?

Adrian: Yes, but I am unable to sleep at night because my wife and I are going through a divorce and we were up all last night fighting.

Michael: I understand you have problems at home. Do you see that your tiredness creates danger?

Adrian: Yes. But there is nothing I can do about my divorce.

Michael: I understand. You need to be capable, mentally and physically, if you are going to drive, don't you?

Adrian: Yes.

Michael: So, shouldn't you ensure that you have adequate sleep at night?

Adrian: Yes. But at the moment it is difficult.

Michael: I understand it is difficult, but it is possible for you to find somewhere to rest, isn't it?

Adrian: I suppose. Yes. I could kip down at my mum's.

Michael: Would you sleep better there?

Adrian: Yes. And eat better too.

Michael: So what are you going to do tonight, to resolve this tiredness problem?

Adrian: I will sleep at mum's for two nights. Then I am off for two days. We should have sorted a few things out by then.

Michael: What could happen if you don't sort this situation and you drive whilst too tired to focus your mind?

Adrian: I could end up injuring someone.

Michael: And maybe even worse, right?

Adrian: Yes. Right. Maybe could kill someone.

Michael: So, is this a high priority?

Adrian: Yes. Mike, I will sort it. Thanks.

Michael: Good. Thank you. I am on your side, Adrian.

Adrian: Thanks.

Did you notice how much Mike used questions to make his points?

Questions really are magical linguistic tools, if you use them properly. Did you feel how more easily the conversation flowed with Mike making his important points warmly, but with persistent clarity?

When people are involved in activities that are dangerous or illegal, you have a right, and even a responsibility, to step in and deliver a message that will cause the person to reconsider their current actions.

In the space below, write down three specific examples when you think it would be necessary for you to intervene because of either an illegal activity or a dangerous activity.

Illegal activity	Dangerous activity

Judge right from wrong

In the bible, what does it say about judging others?
'Judge not, lest ye be judged.'

Now, as a manager you do need to make accurate judgments. As a counsellor you probably should not feel compelled to tell people all your judgments.

I want now to make a distinction between two kinds of right and wrong that you should be aware of and be able to distinguish **during a conversation.** (It is important that you do this during the conversation, not two hours after it when you are driving home!)

The distinction is between **knowledge** and **ethical principle.**

Right and wrong in relation to knowledge

Suppose I said, 'Two plus three equals seven.' I would be 'wrong', wouldn't I? Or if someone said, 'Sidney is the capital of Australia,' he would be wrong too. If I said that Napoleon beat Nelson at the battle of Waterloo, again I would be wrong.

But all of these errors are *errors of knowledge*, and do not make me a bad or corrupt person.

Compare the above examples to examples of 'right and wrong' in relation to ethical principle.

If I said, 'It is okay to steal provided you do not get caught,' I would be wrong, wouldn't I?

If you heard a colleague say 'It is okay to fiddle your mileage claim form because lots of people do it,' again that would ethically be wrong. Or if you heard someone say, 'Don't tell her you deleted the file, blame it on Scott. He is new and he will not even know that he didn't do it.' That would be dishonest and wrong, wouldn't it?

The last three examples are breaches of moral principle, not errors of knowledge.

Here is my point :

It is important to be able to distinguish these two types of 'right and wrong'. There are two very different categories of right and wrong.

1   A person can be right or wrong intellectually, i.e. with regard to knowledge, or
2   a person can be right or wrong with regard to ethical principle.

Many people do not make this distinction. It causes them confusion. However, it is a distinction that you the counsellor must be clear on, if you want to be effective.

You must be able to:

1. understand the distinction
2. recognise it when you hear it in conversation
3. challenge people if they are failing to make the distinction
4. have them recognise and act according to their ethical principles.

For example, do you know anyone who gets annoyed if you tell them they have done something (anything!) wrong? It is as if they regard your telling them they have made a mistake as a personal insult.

For example, if you are a woman, you may have had the opportunity to correct a man on his driving. When a woman corrects a man on his driving ability, what generally happens?

For example, if she says, *'I think you took the wrong turn back there, honey. That's three times now you have done it wrong.'*

Does the man generally respond by saying, *'Thank you, for pointing out my error, darling. With that useful information, we will soon be back on track.'*

Or does he say, *'IF YOU THINK YOU CAN DO ANY BETTER, YOU BLOODY DRIVE!'*

Probably the latter.

It is my opinion that 50% of people mistake 'errors of knowledge' as 'personal indictments on their character', and therefore do not take correction and criticism well. They become stubborn and reluctant to change. So as a counsellor/coach, you should approach this issue with caution.

Looking at this point from the opposite side, people often pass off moral breaches as a lack of knowledge, or 'a mistake'.

For example, Albert was caught stealing money from the Christmas fund. When the accountant caught him, this is what he said, *'Everyone makes mistakes, and I am no different from anyone else. You can't condemn me for making an error. I know I was wrong, but who doesn't go wrong sometimes?'*

Another example – I once heard this in a court of law. A man had been found guilty of theft, and his lawyer was making his plea of 'mitigation' The lawyer said, *'My client realises now, that what he did was wrong. It was a terrible mistake that could have happened to any one of us. Nobody is perfect after all.'*

Can you see the cross-over? Albert and the lawyer are attempting to take a conscious ethical breach (dishonesty) and pass it off as an example of inevitable human fallibility, (intellectual error), i.e. from ethical principle to faulty knowledge.

Again, it is clear that these two species of right and wrong are different in kind, and should not be confused. Keep the distinction in mind and be careful about verbalising the word 'wrong'. It is an emotionally charged word.

Instead, keep working with questions to lead people to re-evaluate their perceptions and ask them to generate better options. The new options should be based upon sound knowledge of the facts, tied to correct ethical principles (honesty, integrity, courage).

Judge as good or bad

Not only do people hold differing views of right and wrong, they also disagree about what is good or bad. You may find yourself counselling a person who holds a view very different from yours about something that they regard as good, that you believe is bad. Or vice versa.

The principle to bear in mind here is the same as before: do not verbalise your disagreement over your evaluation of the issue explicitly. Keep it to yourself. But if you feel that people are making errors that will lead them to self destruction or unhappiness, you may challenge their perceptions by means of careful questioning and suggestion, rather than saying outright that the thing they hold to be good, is actually bad.

Consider this example. Rachael is a manager who works in the social services. She leads and manages a group of fourteen social workers that together are called the Independence Support Team. This specialised social work unit helps those people in the community who have social problems and find it difficult to cope with life. Rather than take these people into institutionalised care, they are supported by the team to help keep them functioning in the community.

The job of a social worker working with clients, who are stressed out, is itself a stressful occupation.

Rachael has a colleague Shana who drinks heavily in the evenings and comes to work the following day feeling 'the worse for wear'. The effect of her drinking is beginning to show in the quality and quantity of her work. Rachael has spoken to Shana informally, but Shana said that 'her evenings were her own' and how she chooses to spend them was 'of no business of the management'.

In this dialogue, Rachael has asked to see Shana. She is attempting to approach the subject again but is treading carefully. Notice that the issue of good and bad comes up. Notice how Rachael uses questions extensively to prompt Shana to think about her current habits.

This is how the conversation went.

Rachael: Hi, Shana. Please come in. Thank you for coming to see me. Please take seat. Would you like a coffee?

Shana: Thank you. What did you want to see me about?

Rachael: When you came into work this morning, did I hear you say that you were feeling groggy and hung-over?

Shana: I am okay now.

Rachael: On Tuesday last week you were two hours late for work. When you came in, you said you were feeling 'hung over' and later, you went home early in the afternoon.

Shana: Yes. I had an upset stomach. I felt sick.

Rachael: Can you see what I am getting at?

Shana: Yes. You are trying to stick your nose into my business.

Rachael: You went home early because you had a bad stomach. This morning you are hung over. That affects our team ability to provide cover, doesn't it?'

Shana: No. I do my work as well as anyone else. Better than some.'

Rachael: But can you work at your full potential when you are feeling hung over, feeling sick? Can anyone?

Shana: Possibly not. Maybe not.

Rachael: Do you think that drinking in the evenings, then coming to work feeling hung over improves things?

Shana: Well, No. But I am under a lot of pressure and so I like to have a drink in the evenings. It helps me cope with stress.

Rachael: Is drinking your way of coping with stress?

Shana: Yes. Alcohol is good for stress. It calms the nerves. Everyone knows that.

Rachael: As a social worker, have you ever met clients for whom drink has not been good to them. Maybe the reverse, drink has been bad for them?

Shana: Yes, of course.

Rachael: Can you give me one example?

Shana: Yes. Remember Benjamin? He drinks himself into hospital regularly. Drink was the cause of the breakdown of his marriage. That's one of the reasons the family was referred to us.

Rachael: In your work, do you see any examples of drink being bad for people's professional lives?

Shana: Yes. But they overdo the drink. I don't. I use drink to help me relax.

Rachael: In your experience, when does drink turn from being something good in a person's life, to being something bad?

Shana: When it starts to negatively effect their health or relationships or
          work.
Rachael: When you went home last week, feeling ill, wasn't that an
          example of your work being negatively effected?
Shana: Yes, but that was not drink related.
Rachael: When you came in this morning feeling hung over, were your
          powers of concentration good or less than good?
Shana: Well, I was okay after a short while. Look, what are you getting at?
Rachael: Can't you tell?
Shana: You are on my back again, trying to tell me what to do in my own
          time.
Rachael: Or could I be asking you to look again at the effect that drink may
          be having on your work. Could it be that what you think is good,
          is not good? Is that at least possible?
Shana: (Pause) It is possible. But it is my business not yours.
Rachael: Do people sometimes do things because they feel good, even
          though, in fact, they are bad?
Shana·   I know what you mean. But this is not one of them.
Rachael: Would you check in your mind to see if that is still true? Could
          you be missing something?
Shana: (Thoughtful silence)
Rachael: Could it be that drink might be harming you, not helping you.
          Might it sometimes be bad, not good?
Shana: (Thoughtful silence)
Rachael: Would you think on it?
Shana: Yes. I will.
Rachael: If you want to talk to someone about stress management, I can
          refer you. And if you want to talk to me about your caseload, you
          can talk to me. You know that, don't you?
Shana: Yes. Is that all?
Rachael: Yes. By the way, how is Joanne getting on with that new housing
          project........'

Although Rachael did not get a firm commitment from Shana to
change her drinking habits, what do you think she did achieve?

In the space below, write down what you think Rachael achieved
by her intervention, and also, write a note on how she did it.

Do it now.

Two things Rachael achieved

1

2

Two observations on her method

1

2

Six points to ponder

1. **You have to think and judge.**

2. **Judge right from wrong (distinguish an ethical breach from errors of knowledge).**

3. **Judge good from bad.**

4. **Judge safe from dangerous.**

5. **But be careful of the way you communicate those judgments.**

6. **Work implicitly.**

Step by step

The clarity/reason/emotion model

Steps

I want now to discuss with you a framework that will help you in a counselling session. All consistent, effective action is structured. So if you want to be a consistently effective counsellor, work using a structure.

The structure I want to show you has three main elements. The three key elements are:

✓ clarity
✓ reason
✓ emotion.

Briefly this means, in order to achieve happiness and peace of mind, people have to have three things in place:

1. a sense of **clarity** about their personal goals and standards
2. a **rational method** (a plan) for achieving their goals and/or standards (1)
3. a **positive emotional balance** that will give them the motivation and energy to put the plan (2) into action to achieve their goals.

These three steps have sub-categories, to be sure, but everything depends on these three key concepts, taken in order. The reason many people need your counselling help is that they have one or more elements of this basic formula missing, i.e.:

1. they do not know specifically what they want ... and /or
2. they are unsure of what standards they should live by or expect from others ... and /or
3. they do not have a workable plan ... and /or
4. they do not have the resources to put their plan into action ... and /or
5. they have a goal, a plan and the resources, but they lack the emotional power, the confidence, motivation, enthusiasm to make it happen.

Your goal is to identify what bits of the puzzle are missing and help the person construct the full set.

You can do this by:

1. understanding the elements of the model
2. using your questioning technique to identify what bits the person has, and what he does not have
3. building upon his strengths
4. building up his weaknesses.

Let's start. Step one is to have a look at the following diagram. It shows the structure.

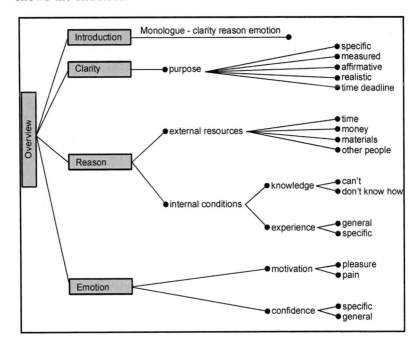

The first stage of the counselling session is the introduction.

The introduction is a period where your task is to settle the other person's nerves, remove any fear and outline the framework for the session. Your introduction might start with 'the social niceties'. This would include greetings and asking the person if they would like a seat, a cup of tea – things of that nature.

Then the introduction proper begins when you, the counsellor, sketch out the clarity/reason/emotion (CRE) model). The way I do this is to say something like:

'Thanks again for coming in. Chris, in my experience there are three things that can stop people achieving their goals -

1 they don't know exactly what their goal is, or

2 they have a goal, but do not have a plan or the resources to achieve their goal, or

3 they have a goal and the resources, but they have a bad feeling, or a fear that stops them.

I want to help you. So what I would like to do in the next half hour is to go through these three elements and help you to figure out what your next steps are. Is that okay?'

What is the purpose of this monologue?

The purpose of this monologue is simple. It is to settle the other person's mind by providing him or her with a broad plan for the session. The wording is vague enough to cover practically every situation, yet meaningful enough to act as a mental agenda.

You can see that the first item of the CRE model is 'Clarity of purpose'. This is the most important part, because the rest of the discussion is an attempt to work out how to attain their intended purpose.

Counselling principle – remember the following sentence forever.

 Purpose is the root of success and happiness.

'Success' is not won by fleeting moments of sensory pleasure. We cannot gain happiness by blindly filling life with pleasure, by eating huge quantities of our favourite foods or drinking crates of fine wine or taking pleasure-enhancing drugs. Many people have tried to achieve happiness by taking the taking the 'sensory route', but lose everything along the way.

No. Happiness is more complex and elusive than that. Your happiness flows whenever you have the realisation that you have achieved one of your goals.

Happiness requires the achievement of a valued purpose.

Similarly,

Purpose is the root of success.

Success can be defined as 'the achievement of a pre-determined purpose'.

To feel successful, you have to reach or fulfil a goal, to which you attach an emotional value. And it is impossible to achieve a goal that does not exist. Therefore the pre-condition of feeling successful is having a purpose.

Since 'Clarity of purpose' is such an important concept, I want to break off and discuss it as a separate topic.

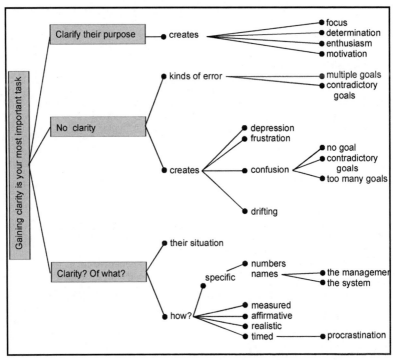

Clarity of purpose is the trigger of emotions

Why is clarity of purpose so important? Because having clarity or purpose causes many of the positive emotions, and **not having** clarity of purpose is the root cause of many of the negative emotions.

There are many emotional states, or feelings, that flow from having clarity of purpose, and many others that flow from not having clarity of purpose.

Here are a five positive emotional states or feelings that flow directly from achieving Clarity of Purpose.

As you read the list, ask yourself this question, 'Why does this emotion depend on Clarity of Purpose?' The emotions are:

1. Focus
2. Determination
3. Enthusiasm
4. Motivation
5. Inspiration

Focus

'Focus' is the mental act of concentrating on one fixed idea for an extended period. For example, picture an athlete aiming at a gold medal at the next Olympics or the student who sets her mind on gaining an A in her exam. Then contrast that against the person who has a fragmented focus: the stressed office manager who has too many things going on at once.

Or consider the person who has no focus: the lethargic teenager who has not yet formulated any particular aim for his life.

Being focused is an advantage, because then you will concentrate your powers. Being unfocused causes your powers to diffuse.

So you can help people by making them focus.

How do you help people achieve focus?

If a person is focused, it presupposes that his mind has something distinct upon which to focus. Something specific. A goal, an aim or a clearly defined purpose. This purpose rarely impresses itself on the mind from the outside. It has to be consciously selected and acknowledged.

As soon as the decision is made that 'This' is the target, the mind can begin work. The spirit is inflamed with a level of passion impossible to the man who is passively waiting for his sense of purpose to materialise unaided.

This passion is what the person feels as motivation and a higher level of happiness

Determination

If you meet someone who is determined, what does it presuppose? It presupposes that they are determined to achieve something.

Achieve what? Their goal, or purpose. All feelings of determination flow from an earlier decision to achieve some goal, or purpose. Or, to put the same point the other way, all decisions to achieve a purpose result in stronger feelings of determination.

It is impossible to feel the determination without having determined the purpose. If you want to help people to feel more determined, you can do it by asking them to clarify their Purpose.

Enthusiasm

Enthusiasm is another positive emotion everyone wants to feel. You may know someone who is enthusiastic. It rubs off on others and can raise the spirits. You may know people who are the opposite: They drag themselves around. There is no sense of excitement or vitality.

But enthusiasm is not a primary cause. Rather it is an effect that flows from having a clear sense of purpose. If you help people to gain Clarity of Purpose, they will soon discover more intense feelings of enthusiasm.

Remember that enthusiasm is not a genetic trait built into some and denied others. Enthusiasm is an emotion that is available to anyone, provided the correct conditions are in place.

What are the correct conditions?

- Enthusiasm flows in the presence of a compelling goal or purpose.
- Enthusiasm presupposes that there is a goal to be enthusiastic about.
- Enthusiasm without at a goal is impossible.

Let me give an example. The most enthusiastic person I know is a man called Richard. The reason for his enthusiasm is obvious. He is a bodybuilder, and he is always in the process of preparing himself for his next competition. He competes twice every year. So he has his mental sights fixed on one of two goals, either:

- gaining more muscular size and strength, (what he calls 'bulking-up') or ...
- reducing and refining his body, down towards his competition weight where all the fat is stripped away to reveal his muscles. (He calls this reducing phase 'ripping up').

So Richard is always focused on making progress – either getting bigger or getting smaller, at different times of the year.

I asked Richard why he put himself through all the hard training and dieting for what seemed like no reward.

He smiled and said, *'You are thinking of rewards only in financial terms, Chris. You are right that bodybuilding does not make me much money. It does much more than that. It gives me a purpose. It feeds my soul. Without something to aim for, I would lose my zest for life and my enthusiasm.'*

I couldn't have put it better myself..

 If you want to instill enthusiasm in people, help them to discover an exciting, clear purpose.

Motivation

Motivation is another positive emotion that is akin to enthusiasm. A feeling of motivation is the spark that turns enthusiasm into practical action.

Motivation is another high value emotion that people want to experience. But they cannot get it by will power. It is not a primary cause. It is a secondary effect of having a clear purpose in mind.

Think for a moment about the word 'motivation'. The word has its roots in the word 'motive'. What does that tell you? It says that, to get motivation, you need first to have a motive (a purpose, a goal).

Motivation in the absence of a motive is impossible.

So ask yourself this question, 'If motivation comes as a direct result of having a goal, how can I help others find their motivation?' Answer – by helping them formulate their goals and clarify their purpose.

A clear motive creates a potent motivation

The lack of clarity of purpose creates negative emotions

Just as clarity of purpose is the starting point of the important positive emotions, a lack of purpose is the starting point of many important negative emotions.

There are four negative emotions that flow as a direct consequence of not having clarity of purpose

Drifting

Drifting and aimlessness are the most obvious signs that a person does not have a clear purpose. There will be times when people will come to you for your guidance, because they feel 'fed up'. They are unhappy but do not know why.

Often it is because they have not got anything 'in front' of them to spur them on, emotionally. They are like a ship in the doldrums, drifting without a goal, plan or enthusiasm. This feeling may be in spite of the fact that they are in a good position; they are well educated and are blessed with huge potential. But they are not focused on anything particular and so they are drifting.

Drifting results from not having a purpose. So if you want to help someone out of the doldrums, what should you do?

 Have a person realise when he is drifting.

Confusion

Confusion can come one of three varieties:

1. confusion from having no goal
2. confusion born from having too many goals
3. confusion born from having contradictory goals.

1 Confusion born from having no goal

If people are in the state of drifting as a result of having no goal, they will often feel confused. They will feel confused because they will not understand why they are unhappy. When they look at their situation, they will have to admit that there is nothing to complain about, but still they feel unfulfilled.

For example, I have a friend called Jenny, who was married with two wonderful teenage children, a boy and a girl. Her husband runs an extremely successful business and they have attained financial success.

Jenny lived in a large house and drove an expensive car. She worked the mornings, part time in the business, and looked after the house and family in the afternoons. She had domestic help with the housework and a gardener called twice per week to tend to the grounds. Yet still Jenny felt depressed, aimless and even useless!

I was asked to counsel her because her husband could not understand why Jenny could be so unhappy, when she had a situation that most people would describe as ideal.

Jenny could not convince herself that she had 'anything to be unhappy about.' She felt bad, and confused because she could not explain her negative emotions. As a result, she began to feel guilty about feeling bad. Which made her feel worse!

She was in the land of milk and honey and was feeling wretched.

But if you understand that emotions flow as a consequence of clarity of purpose, I expect you could put forward a theory that would explain Jenny's reaction.

In the space below, making use of the idea of **clarity of purpose**, explain your theory as to why Jenny felt bad, in spite of 'having everything'.

Secondly, how would you help Jenny to regain her spirits?

```
Jenny felt bad because:




```

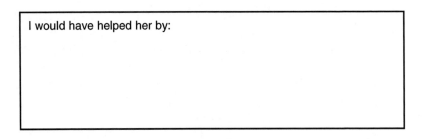

I am hoping you wrote that Jenny was feeling bad because she lacked her own clear purpose. She was feeling bad, because she was drifting.

All her material needs were apparently taken care of. There was, however, one hidden need. That was that Jenny needed her own sense of purpose – something upon which to focus her mental and emotional energy.

To help her, I had her define a valuable, personal goal, one that was hers, not an extension of someone else, (not related to her husband's business, nor her children's education). Jenny decided to go back to nursing. That was something she had been trained for. She had given up her career when her husband's success no longer made her career financially necessary to the family.

Within a month of finding her purpose, Jenny was again on top form, to everyone's benefit.

 Help people to overcome unhappiness by showing them how to focus on a personal goal.

2 Confusion born from having too many goals

As you have just read, confusion can be born from having no purpose. But, it can also flow from having too many goals.

I have personally fallen foul of this principle. I know the value of having well defined purpose statements and goals, so I sometimes over-do a good thing. I set too many! I want to be a super-weight lifter, author, corporate trainer, businessman, artist, father, world-traveller, musician, historian and millionaire playboy. All at the same time!

As a consequence, I have a tendency to have a split focus, rather than concentrated focus. As a result of that, I become confused and sometimes de-motivated, because no matter how many goals I am achieving, I am failing to achieve one of my other goals.

For example, as I am sitting down to write this page, I am bemoaning the fact that I have not practiced my classical guitar for three days and I not yet revised my notes for a corporate training day I am scheduled to do next week.

Having too many targets at the same time leaves me in a state of overwhelm. Then I need counselling! If you were my counsellor, and you were going to help me out of this situation, what would you do?

In the space below, write out your plan for our counselling session.

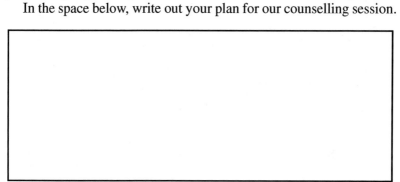

Sometimes I recognise the problem and I talk to myself. I tell myself that although having clear goals is essential, I must also have a hierarchy of goals. I have to know which goals take precedence over which. I do not have the time or energy do everything, but I do have the time to do the most important things.

So clarity of purpose also includes the ability to:

- be clear of the relative hierarchical value of all the goals in life at any particular time
- act in accordance with the highest priority items and not be swayed by trivia.

When people do not know the relative values of their goals, or they act against their priorities, they fail to find either success or happiness.

Help people to find success, help them organise their priorities and encourage them to act in accordance with them.

3 Confusion born from having contradictory goals

If people have clear, well-organised goals, but still find confusion, it is because they have contradictory goals.

Contradictory goals are opposite goals. They are goals that oppose each other. Contradictory goals spell trouble!

People who have contradictory goals find that the attainment of one goal necessitates the failure of another. Contradictory goals are a recipe for emotional turmoil and upset.

For example, Thomas wanted to spend all his evenings relaxing with his girlfriend, and at the same time wanted to earn his degree in higher mathematics. One goal required lots of quality time with Angela, the other lots of quality time with algebra.

As counsellors, what should we do to help Thomas?

We should help him to decide the priorities, or find some other way of resolving the contradiction.

Have him discover which one of these goals takes precedence or, find a way to integrate the two goals so that they do not oppose each other. For example, could Thomas persuade Angela to take the class with him?

Emily wanted to give up her paid employment to start her own business, and at the same time, she wanted the security of having a regular income with sick benefits and paid holidays.

As a counsellor, what should we do to help Emily? We should help her to decide the priorities, or find some other way of removing the contradictions.

Contradictions break the laws of logic. Contradictions cause confusion, anxiety and unhappiness.

 Help others to identify and resolve their contradictions.

Frustration

Frustration is another consequence for a person who does not have clarity of purpose. People feel frustrated when they know, deep down that they have more inside them than they are currently expressing.

Many people are under-achieving. They are not expressing their full potential and they can feel the tension inside. It is as if unused potential is trying to burst out of them, and the person is having to repress it. This causes an internal pressure that the person feels as frustration.

If, as a manager, you want to help people to regain their composure and overcome frustration, one way to do it is help them identify and clarify their purpose.

 Help the people discover a purpose that will allow them to express their full potential.

Depression

People are unhappy when they do not achieve their goals. A certain way to not achieve a goal is to not to have one. Do you know how many people there are who feel depressed, feel unproductive, simply because they have not discovered an exciting 'purpose'?

People feel happy whenever they achieve their goals. In order for people to achieve their goals, they must know what they are.

Happy people are happy, because they know their goals and are striving to achieve them.

 Guide people to find out want they want.

After that lengthy debate, we are certain that we must help the person achieve that state of 'clarity of purpose'.

Let us talk about how to go about it.

Purpose through S M A R T targets

Preview of this section

- Define the current situation.
- Define what people want.
- Learn SMART targets.
- Help people gain clarity by asking them to quantify their goals numerically.
- Identify specific people.

Your task is to gain clarity on two issues:

- the current situation
- their future goals.

Let us take these two sub-sets, one by one.

Clarity about the current situation

If you are lost, what is the most urgent missing information you need to discover? Your present location. If you do not know where you are now, what are your chances of finding your way home?

So, the first priority for you, as a counsellor is to have the other person explain his or her current situation. As you ask the person to explain the situation, separate out what is said into two broad categories: **facts and feelings**

Your first task is to understand the situation in terms of the facts, and then to understand the emotional feelings that flow from the individuals' interpretation of the facts.

But, be clear on this point, you must get to the facts. Try not to get too tangled up in their interpretations and feelings at this point. You need to gain a clear perspective on the current situation, and in so doing, you will be helping the person to avoid 'not seeing the woods for the trees'.

Frequently, this act of having people untangle their feelings from the facts confronting them is enough for the solution to become apparent.

I have had the situation when the counselling session finished at this point. I did not need to do any more for the person. The act of identifying the factual situation and distinguishing it from the emotional situation was in itself, all the help the person needed.

In order to do this, remember the principle of objectivity.

Keep in mind the distinction between objective and subjective language and, at this point, be like a police detective who needs to know the objective facts-of-the-case before they can do any intuitive, deductive or creative thinking.

Be ready to take written notes and 'map out' what the person is telling you onto paper, so that you can build up a clear and distinct mental, verbal picture of the persons situation. When you have done that, you are ready for the next sub-step (the second element of clarity)

Want does the person want?

Your next task is to help the other person to clarify, specifically, what he wants. Help him achieve 'clarity of purpose'.

Every one feels better when they have a purpose. Everyone feels worse when they lack purpose. It is a fundamental psychological need to have a sense of certainty. People without a purpose are literally aimless – drifting emotionally and intellectually.

Some people feel confused and unsure because although they are clear about what they do not like, they do not know what they would have instead. As a result, they lack purpose.

For example, have you ever heard someone say, *'I can't stand my job. I dread Monday mornings.'*

That person is clear about what he does *not like*, but what is he not yet clear about? He is not yet clear about what he would do instead.

A negative goal (a 'not-this' goal) is not real. 'Not this!' is not enough. Your mind needs to know, 'If not this, then what?'

In 2003, I worked with a police officer, Andrew who was demotivated and disheartened with his job. He would tell me (for hours) about all the things he did not like about his role – the stress, the shifts, the paperwork, the uncomfortable uniform and so on. I realised that he had extreme clarity about what he *did not like* about his current situation, but when I asked, *'What do you intend to do instead?'* his answer was less clear.

He said, *'I don't know. Maybe run a pub somewhere. Or set up my*

own business. Be self employed.'
   'Self employed doing what?' I enquired.
   Andrew looked up and said vaguely, *'I don't know.'*
   Andrew knew all the things about his current situation that he did not like, but what was he missing? He didn't know what he did want.

Desired situation formulated as a SMART target

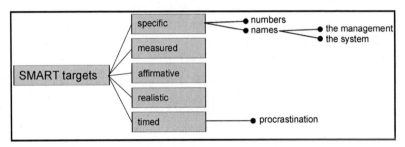

The next step to helping a person achieve success is to clearly define what 'success' means for that individual.
   So, your task as a counsellor is to have the person crystallise their vague wishes and desires into specific tangible SMART targets.
   SMART is a mnemonic that will help you to remember the five criteria against which the goal must be compared. In order to achieve clarity the goal should be:

  1. **Specific**
    2. **Measured**
      3. **Affirmative**
        4. **Realistic**
          5. **Time limited**

Let us look at these, one by one:

Specific (Smart)

When you are counselling, encourage people to be as specific as possible. Vague, ill-defined statements have no power to inspire.
   Imagine that you were acting as my counsellor. During our conversation you asked me, *'What do you want, Chris?'*

If I said, *'I want what everyone wants. I want to be happy,'* what would be the problem with that statement? It would be questionable because, 'to be happy' is too vague.

So, what would your next question be?

Maybe you might ask, *'What specifically would make you happy?'*

If I said, *'I want to save more money this year than last year,'* is that specific?

No. It is not specific enough, because 'more money' can mean any amount. Did I mean one pound more? One thousand pounds more? What would you have to ask me to help me achieve clarity? The conversation might continue like this.

You: Specifically how much more, as a percentage, would you say was right?
Me: Oh, I don't know.
You: Approximately, then. Give me a range. How much more do you think?
Me: Maybe twenty to thirty percent more.
You: Twenty to thirty percent. Good. Now, you are making progress.

How can you be sure when a person is being 'specific'? You can be sure only by listening carefully to their language. There are two things to listen out for – **numbers and names.**

Listen out for numbers

Have the person quantify vague statements by asking for numerical values. These may be in the form of rates, percentages (as above example illustrates), ratios, dates, times or fractions.

For example, in the leisure centre fitness room, two brothers, Aaron and Brian, were discussing with me whether they should set the goal of 'getting into shape'.

I asked Aaron, *'What do you mean by 'get in shape'?'*

Aaron said, *'Well you know, "get in shape" means what it says. I've been talking about it for years, but never managed it. This is the time!'*

Then I turned to Brian and asked, *'When you say, "get in shape", Brian, what does it mean?'*

Brian said, *'I mean that I intend to lose exactly one stone of bodyweight by April the first. I want to reduce my waist measurement from 40" down to 34" and I want to do that by going on a 1,800 calorie per day diet and running two miles, three times per week.'*

Now, which of the two do you think will be more motivated and enthusiastic? Brian of course.

Why? Because his thinking is that much more advanced. He has solidified his vague initial goal by applying numerical values to it.

 Ask people to quantify their goals numerically.

Listen out for names

Ask the person you are counselling to be precise when he is talking about people. If he has goals that relate to others, make sure that he specifies exactly whom he is referring to.

Specifically, listen out for words that imply that the person is thinking that a group of people is equivalent to a singular being. When you hear the person you are counselling talking about a group as if the group were a single entity with a purpose, then consider questioning to gain more detail.

For example, a common word to listen for when counselling is the unspecified 'they', as in the following:

'They say that things are going to get worse next year.'
'They are out to get me.'
'They say that they are going to make redundancies.'

Who is this mysterious 'they'?

Your task as a counsellor is to help the person become clearer in the thinking processes, and one way is to have the person think carefully about who he or she means when using the unspecified 'they'.

Here is an example.

Louis: Chris, I would like to leave my current position and set up my own small business, but you know what they say – business is bad at the moment.

Me: When you say, 'they say business is bad', who do you mean?

Louis: Those people in the media and people generally?

Me:	Who are you talking about, Louis? What do 'they' know about you or your idea?
Louis:	I not sure exactly who said it. I just have heard it said – that's all.
Me:	So you have heard it said by someone, somewhere. Is that really enough to stop you and your plan?
Louis:	No. I suppose not. don't know why I said it.

In this case, Louis had a vague fear that was unsupported by any definite evidence. By challenging Louis's use of the unspecified 'they', I brought it home to him that he was thinking without clarity.

There are other common, unspecified groups that you should listen out for. Here are two more common concepts that need to be specified, if you hear them used.

- the system
- the management.

If you hear them, you may want to question the person to have him gain greater clarity. Have the person identify the specific individuals behind the generalisation. If they are able to name the specifics, they gain clarity, if they cannot, they may realise, as Louis did, that that portion of their thinking is unclear.

'The system' is a universal, ill-defined concept that can create poor thinking. When counselling, it is often useful to have the person check himself by asking him to specify whom, in particular he means when he refers to 'the system' (after all, the system is a system of individuals and their procedures).

Here is an example of how a conversation might sound.

Jeremy:	You know, I would get my tax sorted if I could, but I can't because 'the system' works against me!
You:	Who in the system is against you?
Jeremy:	Pardon ... What do you mean?
You:	Who specifically in the system is against you?
Jeremy:	Nobody as such, I suppose. It is just that I do not know which department is responsible for my application.

In the last example, the 'system' needs to be unmasked. Jeremy sees 'the system' as an impersonal, powerful entity that operates in mysterious ways to stop him, or keep him from achieving his goals.

I know more than one Jeremy-type. We need to help people to break through this particular fear by asking them to put individual people back into the picture, thus making 'the system' at once, both more human and smaller.

The management is another unspecified phrase that people use frequently in business counselling sessions, as the source of their problems or as an entity with God-like powers.

When you hear people using 'the management' as an unspecified general name, it is often useful to ask them to specify the term more accurately.

It might sound like this.

Georgina: The management here is useless. They do not care about us.

You:　　Who specifically, in the management team, does not care about you?

Georgina: Mr Moore for one! He told me he didn't care whether I had a dental appointment; I was not allowed to go home early.

You:　　So when you say "the management" doesn't care', do you really mean, Mr Moore wouldn't let you have more time off?

Georgina: Yes. The others are okay. But he really has a bad attitude.'

In this case, Georgina did have a particular manager (Mr Moore) and a particular event (being refused time off) in mind, but she had allowed that event to become a generalisation that referred to the whole management team and to refer to every circumstance.

By asking Georgina to specify whom she meant, her thinking was reconnected to her actual experience.

 Reconnect people to their experience. It is always helpful.

Measured (sMart)

Another aspect of clarity you can use to help people is 'measurable' goals. In one sense, this aspect is contained in the previous step. We have already talked about making outcome numerically specific – and that will make the goal measurable. But measured means more that being able to quantify a goal or outcome.

You may want to ask the person to consciously choose what will be the measure of success. In other words, ask the person what criteria will he use to know whether or not he has achieved his goal.

Let me illustrate what I mean. Recall the example of Brian and Aaron who both had the goal of 'getting in shape'? Brian had specified his goal as losing exactly one stone of bodyweight by April the first. Also reducing his waist measurement from 40" down to 34", eating 1,800 calories per day and running two miles, three times per week.

Of all the things that Brian might measure, which ones is he actually going to measure?

To be effective, people need accurate information that tells them about their progress. Psychologists call this information 'feedback'. In order to get feedback, the person must decide, in advance, what he should 'track'. What should he pay attention to?

For example, a conversation with Brian might go like this.

You: Brian, of all the things you could measure, which ones are you actually going to measure? Your weight, your running times, your waist measurement ...?

Brian: Probably my bodyweight and waist measurement.

You: Are you not intending to measure your daily calories or running times?

Brian: No. I want to lose weight. Running is just my way of doing it. But I am not doing this to become an athlete.

You: Who is going to measure you?

Brian: I will measure myself.

You: How often will you weigh yourself?

Brian: Once per week, on Sunday. In the morning, before breakfast.

You: Brian, I am impressed with your planning.

Ask the people you are counselling:
- **How will you know when you are winning?**
- **What are you going to measure?**
- **In what way will you measure?**
- **How frequently should you check? Every day, every week?**

Affirmative (smArt)

Goals should be stated in the affirmative sense. We discussed this point in the first part of the book. Many people make negative goals, by naming what they do not want.

Knowing what you do not want is not enough. More important for you is to help people to think about what they do want. Have them tell you their affirmative goals, because as they tell you, they are telling themselves too.

Listen carefully and notice if people name negative goals – not to have X or not to put up with Y any more.

Try to have people state what they do want, in a positive, affirmative statement.

Here is a recent example from my notes:

James: I do not want to be in my job this time next year.

Me: What exactly is your job now?

James: I am working at a school doing some administration.

Me: What do you want to do instead?

James: Anything but that!

Me: Knowing what you do not want is not enough. It leaves completely unclear what you do want. So you do not have anything specific to aim at. What kind of job would inspire you and allow you to earn enough money?

James: I used to work in a garden centre as a sales person. I was good at it. I would like to get back to being in sales or marketing.

Me: Where could you find out about marketing or sales jobs?

James: There is a recruitment agency in town with lots of sales and marketing cards in the window.

Me: When are they open?

James: Monday through to Saturday. Why?

Me: When do you think you might visit the agency?
James: I'll go tomorrow during my lunch break.

When you reach the end of this paragraph, read the above scene again. This time notice how quickly I moved James away from talking about what he does not want, to talking about what he would replace it with.

Notice too, how quickly the conversation moves to ways in which James is thinking about the steps to achieve his goal. We moved from the negative to the affirmative. When you are counselling, do the same thing; focus on the affirmative.

 Have people talk about the future in affirmative language.

Realistic (sma**R**t)

Help the person to relate goals and expectations to reality.

Sometimes people are too optimistic – sometimes they are too pessimistic.

Our goal as a counsellor is to be, a **'rational optimist'**, a person who is primarily rational, objective and realistic, and then adds a degree of optimism.

It pays to be optimistic. **Optimism** is a habitual way of evaluating events that assumes success will come. That assumption is maintained unless something specific and concrete is present to doubt it.

Pessimism is the opposite: it is a habitual way of evaluating events that assumes that things will go wrong. Many people are pessimistic. They believe in Murphy's Law – that whatever can go wrong *will* go wrong.

Having realistic goals is obviously an advantage. However, a too strict interpretation of what is achievable may limit the creativity. So I also recommend being an optimist. A 'rational optimist' assumes the best reasonable interpretation that the facts will allow.

It will be helpful for you to assume the mental attitude of a 'rational optimist' as you counsel others.

What are the alternatives?

You could be a counsellor with the attitude of a 'blind optimist'. If you decide to be an over-optimistic counsellor, what will be the painful consequences?

If you are an over-optimistic counsellor, you may not call the person's attention to facts that will later cause problems. If you are too optimistic you will assume certain things will happen without the evidence to support that belief. As a result, you will not ask enough critical questions to inspire a more logical evaluation of the situation.

For example, many people who start up a small business enterprise are optimistic. They have to be. But sometimes they are over optimistic. They over--estimate their first year's sales. They have too rosy a picture of the demand that their product will inspire. Budding business entrepreneurs assume that eager customers the world over will beat a path to their door. Optimism is good, but over-optimism has been the cause of many failures. Therefore as a business counsellor and coach, be a rational optimist – an optimist with a talent for critical analysis.

Or, if you are a counsellor who is too pessimistic, you may inadvertently underestimate people's potential. If you underestimate a person's growth potential, you may ask too many critical questions. Asking too many critical questions can shake the confidence of people who cannot read the future.

Because they cannot be 100% certain that things will turn out right for them, too many critical questions can raise too many unanswerable doubts. As a result, you the counsellor may inadvertently stifle a great plan; one that would have worked but was never put into practice.

A good counsellor is aware and conscious of the correct level of optimism and pessimism.

 Be a 'rational optimist'.

Time limit (smar**T**)

Learn to have people name a time limit. It will help them to beat procrastination. If you do not ask people to consider the time deadline by which they expect to have achieved their goal, there is a danger that some will procrastinate.

I define 'procrastination' as 'the habit of putting off the things you know you should do, because you do not want to do them'.

Without a deadline, people will always have the opportunity to say, 'I'll start tomorrow.' With a deadline, even a self-imposed one, there is a certain pressure, a feeling of urgency that may impel people to take action. When you are helping other people to clarify their ideas about what they want to achieve, ask them to set a time limit, a mental deadline for its accomplishment. If you forget, they will not think to impose a deadline, and so they will put things off.

I can illustrate the power of a deadline by referring you to the example of completing this book.

When James Alexander asked me to write this book, he gave me a sheet of paper outlining our agreement. On that paper was written a series of deadlines, one of which was that the book should be in such a state of readiness that it would be possible to do the cover designs and the advertising leaflets.

That deadline was late November. As I write this, it is mid-September. So I have less than two months. I can feel the pressure of the deadline beginning to motivate me to 'buckle down' and do the necessary work.

Remember, without the pressure of a deadline, some people procrastinate. As a counsellor, you must be on the lookout for signs of the person wishing to procrastinate.

To help them to stop, ask them about their deadlines.

 Ask people to set time limits for themselves.

That concludes the first element of our counselling model. Here is a quick review of the principles we have discovered in the last section.

- **If you want to instil enthusiasm in people, help them to discover an exciting, clear purpose.**

- **In order to help people find success, help them organise their priorities and encourage them to act in accordance with them.**

- **Help others to identify and resolve their contradictions.**

- **Help the people discover a purpose that will allow them to express their full potential.**

- **Ask them to quantify their goals numerically.**

- **Reconnect people to their experience. It is always helpful.**

- **Ask the people you are counselling, 'How specifically will you know when you are winning?'**

- **Have them talk about the future in affirmative language.**

- **Be a 'rational optimist'.**

- **Ask people to set time limits for themselves.**

Helping the person you are counselling to decide a goal is a great start, but it is not enough.

People will need your help to organise a practical plan – one that stands a good chance of success. So now, have them use their **powers of reason** to think logically about what resources they will need.

That is your next step – so turn the page and keep reading.

Counselling to invoke the use of reason

What is 'reason'?

In this context, 'reason' means the logical mind. The ability to see the facts as they are, independent of wishes or fears, together with the ability to integrate the facts into a workable plan of action.

Reason is the distinguishing evolutionary characteristic. It is mankind's means of survival. It is our rational and logical abilities that separate us from other animals on the planet. The fact that people can think rationally does not necessarily mean that they always do.

If we are to assist others, we must bring Reason to the problems that the person perceives.

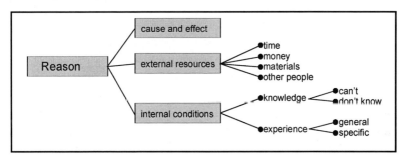

Logic is the method of reason. The ability to think logically about the other's situation, goals and desires is the essence of this method. The ability to apply logic to solve problems is crucial because we have to comply with the facts,

Logic is defined as **'the art of non-contradictory thinking'**. In other words, people think logically when they think in ways that do not contradict (a) the facts, (b) the laws of nature or (c) their other ideas.

If a person you are counselling is thinking in ways that do contradict the facts, the laws of nature or their own principles, then that person needs help. Why?

Because we live in a world of **cause and effect**.

In order to achieve any effect, we must initiate specific causes. One cannot expect an effect to take place without initiating the requisite causes. For example, a person cannot expect to pass an exam (the effect), without initiating the cause (intelligent study).

Similarly, one cannot initiate a cause and escape the effect. For example, if Steve increases his spending on his credit card (a cause), he should not be upset when he receives a bill for the interest (the effect).

Our goal as a counsellor is to help people to apply reason and logic to their situation in an attempt to work out the best way forward.

 Think logically and base plans on facts not wishes or fears.

Cause and effect

When we are applying reason to a situation, we are relying on the logical principle of cause and effect.

The law of cause and effect cannot be breached. It is a fundamental law of nature. If we want a particular effect, we must first enact the proper causes. If we want to halt or prevent a particular effect, we must identify its cause, and interrupt it. If we take away the cause, the effect ceases.

This seems so obvious as to be almost self-evident.

But the sad truth is that many people ignore cause and effect.

1. Some want effects without causes. For example, some people want to make more money, but may not want to do make any extra effort (wishing for an effect without cause).

2. Others initiate causes and hope they will not get the effects. For example, a person may smoke forty cigarettes a day, eat massive quantities of junk food then be surprised when he doesn't feel well. He hopes that he can initiate causes (poor health habits) and then avoid the effects (poor health).

As a professional counsellor, be on the lookout for both kinds of error.

If we want to help people, then we must help them set the conditions whereby the effect that they want becomes the consequences of the causes they enact.

There are two categories of logical conditions and causes we must help the person to consider.

- **Internal conditions** – the resources inside the individual concerned. These are:

  1 Knowledge
  2 Skill
  3 Experience.

- **External conditions.** The resources outside the individual concerned. These are:
  1 Time
  2 Money
  3 Materials
  4 Support from others

Ask questions about each of these aspects. Ensure that the person you are talking to has considered all the elements needed to progress.

Let us look at each in turn.

Internal conditions

Internal conditions are 'personal resources'. They refer to the abilities and skills of the person you are coaching.

For example, if Alice wants to achieve a certain result, she must initiate the causes. Some of these causes will require particular personal attributes.

So, as her coach, you may want to ask questions that identify the internal resources she will need:

1 Internal resource of knowledge

Nobody knows everything. There is too much knowledge for one mind to learn. If the people you are working with are not making progress towards their goals, it may be because they lack knowledge. As a result of a lack of knowledge, they are unable to achieve their goal. Then some people say to themselves, 'I can't do it.'

This raises an important point:

Many people have *not* noticed that the words, 'I can't' have two very different possible meanings.

'I can't' can mean both:

- I can't (because it is impossible) and
- I can't (because I do not know how).

For example, recently I was running a management development workshop. We were discussing how people learn new skills. As a metaphor of 'the learning process', we were learning to juggle with three balls,

One delegate, Jane, kept saying, *'I can't juggle. I've never been able to.'* But there was more. There was a non-verbal message in her voice tone that said, *'I've never been able to so I never will be able to!'*

I stopped Jane and asked, *'Why do you keep saying that you can't juggle?'*

She said, *'Because I am clumsy. I have never been any good at juggling. I'll never be able to do this!'*

I asked, *'Has anyone ever taught you a step-by-step method that will guarantee you will be able to juggle?'*

'No.'

' Is it possible that the reason you have not yet learned to juggle is because you do not have a method?'

'Yes. That is very possible.'

'If you keep telling yourself that you can't juggle, that you are clumsy, is that going to help or hinder your learning chances?'

Jane paused, then said, *'Hinder. I understand your point, Chris. From now on I will say, "I can't juggle yet." Better still, "I am learning to juggle".'*

I said, *'Jane, as a general rule, don't say, "I can't." Instead say, "I can, if I have a method."'*

She responded, *'You're right! I will stop telling myself I can't do it, and start telling myself I am learning.'*

 Learn the difference between 'I can't' and 'I don't know how'.

When you hear a person say, 'I can't,' consider asking him, *'When you say, you can't, do you mean that it is impossible for you, or do you mean you do not know how to do it?'*

Some people have not thought about this distinction and consequentially they are too quick to say, 'I can't'. They tell themselves 'I can't' too often and with too much certainty.

This point is important because, when we say, 'I can't', we cut ourselves off from the possibility that we can. We limit the future. We shut down potential.

For example, I cannot run a four-minute mile because I have a damaged ankle (I broke it in a motorcycle accident). A four-minute mile is physiologically impossible for me. I also cannot fill in my year-end tax return. It too is impossible for me, with my current state of knowledge. I will never have a fully functioning ankle, so I will not concern myself with running a four-minute mile. But if I really had to fill in my tax return, I could always take the time to learn what I need.

The same holds true for many activities, skills, talents and abilities that people want or wish they had.

For a typical person, which of the following would fall into the category of 'I can't' and which into 'I can't because I do not know how'?

1 playing the piano
2 making a public presentation
3 breathing unaided, underwater
4 making more money
5 organising paperwork properly
6 managing time more effectively
7 getting into better physical condition.

We probably agree that the only one on the above list that falls into the category of 'I can't' is number 3. The others are all possible, provided you (a) knew how to do it and (b) applied that knowledge.

But how often do you hear people say,
'I can't seem to lose weight.'
'I would love to play a musical instrument, but I can't.'
'I can't seem to manage my time.'
'I can't do maths.'

 Every reasonable desire is possible, provided the person knows what to do!

Our job as counsellors may include having people understand that distinction – i.e. that of separating 'innate ability' and 'knowledge'.

We may need to help someone see that they do have the innate ability, but they lack the knowledge. We help them to identify the specific knowledge they require to achieve their goal and then discover where/how they might find it.

Simple!

The knowledge the person needs may be scientific, legal, procedural, historical, technical, political or psychological.

Whatever it is, it is available and learnable.

Rule for Counsellors

> **As a counsellor and a friend, learn to say this to people:**
>
> *'You can, if you learn how!'*

The internal resource of experience

Experience and knowledge often go together, though they are not synonyms. It is possible to have years of experience and fail to gain knowledge. It is equally possible to have a head crammed full of knowledge and not have the experience to wisely put that knowledge to good use.

Experience can gives the references and background 'common sense' which allow people to better apply whatever conceptual knowledge they have.

You can think of experience as being in two categories – specific and general.

Specific experience

Specific experience is 'contextual experience': limited to a particular field or range. For example, Susan may have lots of practical experience of horses, which would allow her to better put into practice any veterinary knowledge that she might gain through study.

It is possible for a person to be very experienced and confident within their restricted field, but if ever required to move out of their field of expertise, the person feels exposed and uncertain.

General experience

Some people lack the 'general experience' to cope with their problems. 'General experience' is experience gained through living a varied and eventful life. It is not a function of age, but of variety.

Some people leave school at sixteen, win their first office job, and remain at the same post, doing essentially the same thing for forty years. At the end of that time they may have a deep specific level of experience but not necessarily enough experience on a more general level.

Other people change careers and contexts regularly, frequently putting themselves outside their comfort zone. As a result, they gain a broader 'general experience' but maybe at the expense of 'specific experience' in a particular context. They keep 'starting from scratch' which means that though they are 'well rounded individuals' they may lack specific expertise/knowledge in the context they are currently facing.

 As a business counsellor, be ready to distinguish between those who lack 'specific contextual experience' and those who lack 'general life experience'.

What can you do for those people who lack specific experience/ knowledge?

The best way to gain experience is to throw yourself into action and be sensitive to the 'feedback results' your actions are creating.

People who lack specific experience are bound to make more errors than those who have the experience. The key point to remember as a counsellor is to encourage the person to continue taking action, that is, not to allow their lack of experience to create so much apprehension that they freeze up or stand still for fear of making a mistake.

Ask people these questions:

● Isn't action the best remedy for lack of experience?
● Experience comes from taking action, doesn't it?

Encourage the person to continue to take steps and be aware of the inevitable errors. Encourage them not to 'beat themselves up' over their errors, but rather analyse and evaluate the errors and transform them into 'valuable learning experiences'.

This is the best way to approach a lack of experience. Tell people the motto, 'Fake it till you make it' and ask them what it means.

Imagine you faced a difficult situation that was new to you – one in which you lacked experience, maybe a new job role. Within that context, what does the phrase 'Fake it till you make it' mean?

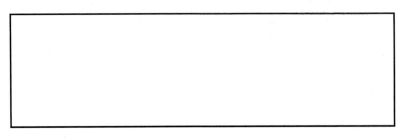

What can you do to help the person who lacks general experience?

This is more difficult because general life experience is non-specific and so, to offer specific help is tricky. The best way I have found is to ask the person to think of a role model – a person who has faced a similar situation and has successfully dealt with it in an ethical and efficient way.

The role model should be someone that the person you are counselling can easily bring to mind and who will act as a guide to action. They do not necessarily have to be personally acquainted with the role model. Film idols, religious, military or political leaders will do.

On the other hand, the individual you are counselling may be able to call to mind a role model who is a personal acquaintance. He may have in mind a perfect role model who happens to be directly accessible. It could be a close friend, a relative or colleague.

Your goal as a counsellor is to help the person who lacks experience to draw from the experiences of others.

Consider saying something like this:

'Other people's experience can be a valuable tool. We can learn by seeing what has worked for others in the past:. We can learn from

other people's victories. We can also learn from what has failed in the past. We can avoid mistakes and errors made by others.

Who do you know who could act as a role model in this situation?'

The key point for you, the counsellor, is that people may not think to use role models unless you ask the specific questions that will trigger the idea.

Let me tell you of an example of how role modelling helped friend of mine.

Lucy is a young mother of two children. She was 27 years old when she had her first child, Scott. Let her take up the story:

'When Scott was born neither my husband nor I had any experience. Scott was born five weeks early and was in special care. I felt overwhelmed by the whole experience of being a parent for the first time. I felt ill equipped and frightened. I didn't know how to change a nappy, feed the baby … I didn't have a clue.

In the special care unit ,I met another mum called Hadie. She was the same age as me, but she was having her fourth child. Because she was on her fourth child, she knew what she was doing. So I glued myself to her for the first two weeks. She was brilliant. I drew from her a lot of her experiences and advice. She really did coach me, Chris. Not only for those two weeks but afterwards as well, when I was at home.

I asked, *'What did you learn from her, Lucy?'*

'She helped me with everything, getting the baby to sleep, learning to distinguish between attention cries and hunger cries. She helped me through the baby blues with her attitude and experience. I learned by watching her with her child, and I learned by asking her questions whenever I was in doubt.'

Then I asked, *'What effect did having a role model have on your feelings?'*

'Oh, it gave me so much more confidence and ability. I was on a speedier learning curve. I learned so much quicker. I didn't have to use trial and error on anything. I didn't have to find out what worked by wading through all the things that didn't work. I went straight to doing the things that do work. I knew they worked because they were tried and tested.'

Finally, I asked, *'So, what would be your advice to anyone in a similar situation, I mean to anyone who is feeling overwhelmed?'*

'Find yourself a role model. Find someone who has been there and done it. Someone who knows what to do and who knows what not to do.'

Have a Hadie!

 Ask people to consider finding a role model.

Rational external resources

To help people achieve their goals, you may have to help them to identify what material resources they will need to gather.

These resources will include some of the following,

1 Time
   2 Money
      3 Materials
         4 Support form others

Rational external resource number one: Time.

Have people organise their thoughts about time. Everyone finds ways to fill each day. It seems to me that everyone believes they are already too busy, and do not have enough time to do the things they need to do.

When you are counselling people towards the achievement of any goal, you may find it helpful to ask them.

'How much time do you need?'
'How much time will this take?
'How will you find the necessary time?'

It may be that the people you are working with will have to think about prioritising competing demands.

For example, right now, as I am writing this, I have three competing demands on my time – I have the goal to write this book, I need to do my weight training, and practice my classical guitar for an examination that is approaching. Each of these goals takes time, a considerable amount of time. I need to negotiate between them.

Many people have the same problem as me. You may have to help them to organise their time priorities.

 Help people to negotiate and arrange their time.

Rational external resource number two: Money

Have people organise their thoughts about money. Many people have goals or outcomes that will require money. As a counsellor, therefore, you should consider asking questions pertaining to money.

You might ask questions such as:

'In order to do X, how much money will you need?'

'You will need to have enough money to do Y, where will you find it?'

Many people have a goal that requires a certain amount of money, but do not take that fact into account. A key task as a counsellor is keeping people connected to reality: And that includes financial reality. Do not allow the people you are working with to evade any relevant fact. Money facts included.

For example, I last year, was working with a man called Roger who had a goal of becoming a gym owner.

During that time, I visited a local auction house, the day before a big auction. The day prior to an auction is the 'viewing day' where one can see the lots and make some buying decisions. On that occasion, I saw a complete set of professional gym equipment for sale. I remembered Roger was looking for an opportunity to set up a gym, so I made a telephone call to his home.

I had a conversation with Roger that went like this:

Chris: Roger, It's Chris. Are you still on the lookout for gym equipment?

Roger: Yes. Why?

Chris: I saw some today. What kind of equipment are you looking for?

Roger: I need professional looking equipment but it needs to be functional, not fancy'

Chris: What do you mean?

Roger: My target group is serious athletes and weight-lifters as opposed to what I call 'keep fitters', so I need heavy, professional equipment.

Chris: Did you know that there is equipment like that available at the Cheltenham auction tomorrow?

Roger: No, I didn't know. How many pieces are there?

Chris: There is a full gym. About fifteen pieces. There are units that look like heavy-duty equipment and some lighter aerobics training equipment. How much money do you have put aside for the equipment?

Roger: Oh, I have a bit.

Chris: Each piece has a reserve of between £300 and £600 pounds. You will need maybe £3,000 to £7,000. Maybe more. Do you have that amount in mind?

Roger: Uh, no.

Chris: How much money do you have available for your goal of opening a gym?

Roger: I have hardly any money. About fifty pounds.

Chris: Can you raise money?

Roger: Not sure. Maybe my mother can lend me some.

Chris: How much do you think you can raise?

Roger: About two hundred.

Chris: Any more?

Roger: Nope!

As you can see, Roger was not thinking straight and was leading himself to frustration because he was evading financial facts and mistaking fantasising for goal setting.

 Keep people in contact with reality, and that includes financial realism.

Rational external resource number three: Materials.

Have people organise their thoughts about materials. The achievement of a goal will usually require some materials. So your duty as a counsellor includes asking questions about the materials they will need to acquire.

The materials may be things such as tools, specialised equipment or new technology. Again, some people evade facts that do not fit into their dreams. As a result, they remain dis-empowered. So you may have to reconnect people with the facts of reality.

Remember to ask people to list the materials they will need. Ask them to be as specific as they can be. Hand them a pen and a piece of paper say, *'What materials will you need? Write down the things you will need?'*

When they have done that, immediately ask, *'What else?'*

The question 'what else?' is sometimes a key question for you. Remember it: *'What else?'*

Keep repeating the question, 'what else ... and what else?' until they have emptied their mind and they finally say, *'That is it! That is everything.'*

This question can stimulate the other person to think of everything they will need to make their goals possible. Then say, *'Good. Now, looking at the list of everything you will need, which things are the most important?'*

Questions like this have the effect of bringing goals and wishes to the level of plans and actions.

 Help transform people's goals into plans.

 Do not let people pretend that the things they need will appear by magic.

Rational external resource number four: the cooperation of other people.

One person alone cannot achieve his goals. We all need help from other people. Why?

- One person does not make an economy.
- One person does not make a family.
- One person does not make a team.
- One person does not make a business.

We live in a society, so we have to be able to gain the cooperation of others if we are to achieve anything worthwhile. Therefore, if we want to achieve anything, we will almost certainly need to gain the cooperation of others.

For example, I have needed help and the co-operation of others to bring this book to you – help from the publishers, help from friends, colleagues, family. I needed the co-operation of people I will never meet – drivers, bookshop owners, merchants and others.

So as a counsellor, help people to turn their minds to the following questions.

'Who can help?'

'Whose assistance do you need to secure?'

You can go even further. Ask additional questions that reinforce the principle of 'mutual co-operation'. Mutual co-operation is the principle that states that all long-lasting, successful relationships are based upon a 'mutual exchange of value'.

One cannot expect to 'receive' for long, without 'giving'. One can expect to gain the long term co-operation of others only if ones gives something in return. If A wants help from B, then A should follow three steps:

- Person A tells person B whose co-operation is needed, exactly **what** kind of help A needs.
- A tells the person B exactly why help is needed.
- A tells the person B exactly what A is willing to do to **repay** the help rendered.

This last point is important but most frequently omitted.

It is important for you to make the point that people cannot expect 'unlimited help for free'. All successful long-term relationships are mutually advantageous. That is, both parties benefit.

A relationship that is one-sided, one where one person does all the giving, and the other all the taking, is unsustainable.

So, whenever people needs to ask for help, remind them to build into the request, some form of 'exchange of value'. Have them consider what they will offer in return for the help.

Remind people that, if they have nothing material to give, they must be sure to offer intangible 'payment' – that is their thanks and gratitude.

Examples of this type of question are:
'If your mother helps you to do this, how can you repay her?'
'If your friend gives you this, what will you do in return?'
'How can you demonstrate your gratitude to your friend for the help?'

 Help people to enlist the cooperation of others in mutually beneficial relationships.

Counselling to inspire the positive emotions

The third category of questions you could ask is related to the emotions. Some people have a goal, they have a plan, and they even have the resources to put the plan into action, but they still do not take the action necessary.

Why? Because they lack they lack motivation or they lack confidence. Emotions are the driving force of action, or inaction. They can help or hinder.

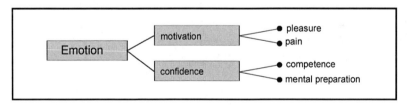

There are certain key emotions that we need to help inspire in others. They are:
- motivation
- confidence

Motivation

Motivation is a positive emotion that flows from having a clear goal (or motive), together with a workable plan. Some people are not motivated because they lack a clear goal, or they have no plan of action (or they lack both).

If you have done the previous steps, you have created the conditions that put into place:

- a clear outcome
- the resources and skills necessary to make it possible.

As a result you may have done enough to inspire feelings of motivation. However, it may be that you have more to do. The person may not be motivated enough to overcome procrastination or fear. So you may have to ask additional questions that will have the effect of boosting motivation.

How do you boost motivation in another person? A good question.

You can do it by recognising the two motivating forces of **pleasure and pain.**

Pleasure is a motivator. People are motivated to act if they think that the action will result in their **achieving a pleasurable benefit**. Pain is a motivator too. People are motivated to act if they think that the action will result in their **avoiding a painful consequence**. Pleasure and pain are powerful motivators.

Advertisers use them both, don't they? Advertisers motivate us to buy particular products by showing us either the pleasurable consequences we will gain if we buy the product, or the painful consequences we will suffer if we do not buy the product.

Advertisers call this the pleasure/pain principle. Can you think of a product that is sold based on the 'pleasure principle'?

Yes, of course – chocolate. Chocolate is a pure 'pleasure product'. Why are people motivated to eat massive quantities of chocolate when they know that it is no good for their figure, their skin or their teeth? The answer is easy – eating chocolate is pleasurable. And pleasure is a motivator, so people are motivated to eat chocolate even when they know it is not good for them.

Advertisers also use the pain principle. The pain principle states 'People will be motivated to act, if they believe that by acting, they will avoid a painful consequence'. So you will be motivated to buy products that you do not want, in order to avoid the painful consequence of not having them. A prime example of something sold to you on the basis of the pain principle is your TV licence. Why do you buy a TV license? To avoid the painful consequences that you will suffer if you do not have one. (The advertising slogan for the state TV licence is 'GET ONE, OR GET DONE!'. Hardly a benefit message filled with positive emotion but it does work to motivate action).

Another 'pain avoidance product' is aspirin. You do not feel a thrill of pleasure when you buy a packet of aspirin do you? No. You buy aspirin to avoid the painful consequences of not having any when you need them.

Because people will act to achieve a pleasurable benefit, or to avoid a painful consequence, you can motivate others by asking 'pleasure/pain questions'.

- All 'pleasure questions' are reformulations of one fundamental question, 'What will be the long term pleasurable benefit you will gain if you do take action?'

- All 'pain questions' reduce down to, 'What will be the long term painful consequences you will suffer if you do nothing?'

By asking both questions in various forms, you will inspire people by both 'the carrot' and 'the stick'. They will see in their mind's eye the benefits of taking action which will create a positive motivation inside. Then, if you ask the right questions, they will see the painful consequences of doing nothing, which will create an emotional 'kick up the pants'- that is a 'negative motivation'.

Some people are motivated by the desire to gain pleasure. Some are more motivated by their desire to avoid pain. By learning to ask questions that inspire a sense of pleasure and pain, you will be able to find ways to boost the levels of motivation in anyone.

For example,I was recently counselling a lady called Olivia. She was working in a low-paid but secure job in the local authority playgroup. She was a single mum, with two children, aged 9 and 11. She was in receipt of certain state benefits and regular 'maintenance' payments from her ex-husband. She was financially solvent, but she felt dissatisfied. She felt dependent. She wanted to be more independent, especially of her ex-husband.

In addition, she felt uneasy because she believed, in her soul, that she was capable of achieving much more than her current levels of (financial) success indicated.

She came to me for counselling. I helped her to identify her goals and the plan.

The goal was to start a marketing company, based in her own home, using the resources she already had. She opened a bank account, set up an office in her spare bedroom, and had her new business cards printed. But then she stopped. She was hesitating and putting off the day when she stopped working for the local authority and started working for herself.

We spoke again and the conversation went like this:

Chris: Olivia, last time we spoke, you had everything ready to go. All the cards were printed, your office was ready and you were intending to tell the playgroup leader you were leaving to begin your one-woman business. But that was weeks ago and you have not made the jump. What is happening?

Olivia: I feel nervous.

Chris: About what?

Olivia: I feel nervous about giving up the security of my regular paid job for the uncertainty of self-employment.

Chris: Do you feel that your business plan is realistic?

Olivia: Yes I do. I only make £100 per week at the playgroup and I think I can immediately double that by working for myself.

Chris: Do you think you have all the materials necessary to make a start?

Olivia: Yes. It is just that I feel nervous about actually committing and cutting myself off from regular, paid work.

Chris: *(moving into my pleasure/pain motivation questions)* Olivia, take a pen and draw a line down the middle of this paper. On one side right 'pleasure' and on the other, write the word 'pain'. Then on the side marked 'pleasure' write down the answers to this question: If you were to go ahead, and make the change, what long-term benefits will you see in the months ahead?

Olivia: In the long term, I will earn more money.

Chris: What else?

Olivia: My income will be uncapped. There will be no set limit on my monthly income.

Chris: Write that down, too. What else?

Olivia: I will be the one controlling my income.

Chris: Good. Write that down. What else?

Olivia: I will gain more self-worth. I want to stand on my own two feet again.

Chris: Right. What else?

Olivia: I think it will be good for the kids to see their mum making a go of things. I think I would be a better role model for them.

Chris: Have you written that down? What other pleasurable benefits do you see?

Olivia: If I make a success of this, my parents would be proud of me.

Chris: Write that down. What else?

Olivia: I would be able to prove my ex-husband was wrong. He said I wouldn't be able to cope on my own. I want to prove I was right!

Chris: Write that one down in big letters! What else?

Olivia: I think the future will open up for me if I can make this work. I don't really know how to say exactly what I mean, but I think things would end up better for me.

Chris: Okay. What else?

Olivia: Nothing else comes to mind.

Chris·   Okay. Now, on the other side of the line, write down at least three answers to this question: What are the painful long-term consequences you might suffer if you did nothing? Doing nothing is an option open to you. You can stay as you are. What will happen if you do nothing?

Olivia: I will continue to be dependent on my ex-husband for money. That makes me feel bad because I do not want to be dependent on him for anything! I will have to stay on benefits, too, which I do not like. I feel like I can and should stand on my own. Plus I will never learn what I am capable of if I do not try. My kids will never see the real me.

Chris: What else?

Olivia: I think that's it.

Chris: Now, Olivia, look at the list. What does it tell you?

Olivia: I can see it.

Chris: You can see what?

Olivia: I can see why I need to do this.

Chris: As you look at the list, and think of the meaning, how does it make you feel?

Olivia: Determined. I am going to do it. And I am going to make it work!

Can you see the process of pleasure/pain questions? Let us review –
the two questions are:

- What are the long-term *pleasurable benefits* you will enjoy *if
  you change*?
- What are the long-term *painful consequences if you do
  nothing* and stay the same (i.e. *do not change*).

Please notice the difference between these motivational pleasure/pain
questions, and the following rational analytical question.

- What are the painful consequences *if you do change*?

Assuming change will be a good idea logically, the person may lack
the emotional courage or motivation to actually make the changes that
the analysis says would be the right thing.

So the motivational questions are designed to give an 'emotional
push'. Check again the first pair of questions above, and then note that
the third question is different. It is different because the purpose of the
third question is to inspire an emotion that will create the action that
the intellect says is the right thing to do.

Both of the motivational questions provide reasons to move. You
may ask these questions to help to motivate another.

 **Learn the pleasure/pain questions and be ready to
use them to inspire action in others.**

Confidence

Confidence is a positive emotion that everyone needs to achieve their
goals. There are two kinds of confidence – **specific and general**.

People feel **'specific confidence'** whenever they feel competent
within a given field or context.

For example, Steve is an engineer and is confident in any similar
practical, hands-on situations. He was recently asked to help in
building an extension to a kitchen area and was very confident about
his abilities to help. But if you put Steve in any context where he is
expected to make public speaking presentation, his confidence is non-
existent.

We all have areas of activity where we feel confident. And we each have other areas where we are less confident. In this regard, confidence relates to competence. If we are competent, we feel confident. If we recognise a lack of competence, it is natural to feel a lack of confidence.

Remedy a lack of 'specific confidence' by improving the knowledge or skills of the person involved.

'General confidence' relates to self-image. It is the 'background level' of confidence a person feels in any context. Some people have high levels of personal confidence and others have a definite lack.

As a coach and counsellor, your job is to boost the general confidence of the people you work with.

Here are two ideas that will help you to boost the confidence of others.

- Build people's confidence with competence.
- Build confidence with preparation.

Build people's confidence with competence

Your first method of boosting a person's confidence is to ask them questions that will have the person feel competent.

To the degree that a person feels competent, equipped and capable, is the degree to which you will inspire confidence in that person. You do that by asking the questions that will have the person tell you how they are (or have been) competent in similar situations.

For example, take Steve as our example of a person who lacks confidence in speaking to others in a formal presentation.

Your task is to have him think of similar situations where he has spoken confidently. It might sound like this:

You: Steve, you have this presentation coming up next week. How are you feeling about it?

Steve: Not good, I am feeling nervous. I hate public speaking.

You: Do you? Many people do. Do you know your material?

Steve: Yes. It is about the new system we have installed. The material is not the problem. I know my stuff. It is just I feel uncomfortable standing up in front of others and presenting.

You: Yesterday at our meeting, when you told Sally and me about your ideas for the presentation, you came across confidently. Why was that?

137

Steve:	Because it was just you and Sally in the room. And it was informal.
You:	Do you remember last month, at John's leaving party, you made a nice speech. You gave him his going away gift. How was that?
Steve:	I wouldn't call it a speech. I just said a few words that is all.
You:	You did a good job of it. I thought you came across well.
Steve:	Did I?
You:	You made a few jokes and told everyone about John's achievements. You came over as a clear speaker then, didn't you?
Steve:	I suppose I did. I never thought of it.
You:	Steve, this morning you were in the office giving the team briefing. You do that nearly every week. How do you do that?
Steve:	The team briefings are different. I know everyone. It doesn't seem like 'public speaking'.
You:	If you present the coming presentation in the same way as you present the team meeting, or as you did at John's leaving party, how would you feel?
Steve:	I would feel fine. But it isn't that easy.
You:	I understand. If you did do it in that spirit, how do you think the presentation would go?
Steve:	If I could treat the presentation as a normal team briefing, it would go well.
You:	Is it possible to rehearse the presentation as normal team meeting? Could you treat it in that way?
Steve:	Maybe.
You:	It would be good, wouldn't it?
Steve:	Better. Yes.
You:	If you did, you would come over well, wouldn't you?
Steve:	Yes. It would be good. Let me work on it. Thanks.

Notice how almost every step is a question that has the other person reinforce their feelings of competence. You can do it by asking for concrete examples of similar situations when similar skills were needed. Your goal is to have the person 'see' in their mind's eye that they already possess the competence to win. With that realisation they gain confidence.

Build people's confidence by building their feelings of competence.

Build confidence with mental preparation and rehearsal

The second method of helping the person gain confidence is through mental preparation and rehearsal.

'Mental preparation and rehearsal' is defined as the act of vividly imagining an event in advance in order to predict and practice the best responses. The practical effect of mental preparation is better performance. The psychological effects of mental preparation is improved confidence.

The reason is that emotions flow from the dominant image in the mind. Mental rehearsal and preparation encourages the mind to be filled with positive images. The positive imagery is the source of the confidence. If people are mentally prepared, they will feel more confidant. If people are not mentally prepared, they will feel uncertain and unsettled.

Let me give you an example how I have used this idea to counsel a colleague. Last year I was working with a new corporate trainer, Terry. He was due to deliver his first full-day training, unaided, to a paying audience. He knew the material but he was feeling nervous.

Terry came to me with his worries.

Terry: I am nervous.
Chris: You know the material don't you?
Terry: Yes. Backwards.
Chris: I have seen you present many times, and you did well. What is happening?
Terry: This time I will be on my own. What if something goes wrong?
Chris: The way to prevent things going wrong is to have a plan.
Terry: I have the lesson plan you sent me.
Chris: Yes. But was my plan for you. I would like you to spend the next half hour alone, and I would like you to work out your plan for *you*. Do this – imagine a perfect training day. Really see it in your mind's eye. Then describe to yourself exactly what you are doing in your imagery. Write down a moment-by-moment, step-by-step description of your best possible performance. Could you do that?

139

Terry: Yes but it might take me more than a half hour.

Chris: Yes. That's okay. See you later.

Two hours later, Terry came to me with four pages of notes with every step of his presentation worked out. He even had notes on what he would do if things went wrong – back-up plans.

I read them through carefully and then turned to him.

Chris: This looks great, Terry. Have these with you tomorrow.

Terry: I will.

Chris: How does having done this mental preparation affect the way you feel?

Terry: It makes all the difference in the world, Chris. For the better. I feel more confident.

Chris: Why?

Terry: Because I know how I want to handle it. That gives me confidence.

Chris: How precisely, did you do the mental preparation?

Terry: I did what you suggested. First I went to a quiet room with my notes and a laptop, and shut the door. I sat down and closed my eyes. I let myself relax. I began to daydream about what I would be like if I was really good. I pictured myself at the venue and in my mind's eye, I was doing a perfect job. Then, periodically, I jotted down the exact things that I felt I had to do to make a good impression, based upon my daydream and imagination.

Chris: What sort of things did you note?

Terry: I noted that I should stand up and move around, not sit down like I sometimes do.

Chris: What else?

Terry: That I should involve the delegates, not to talk for too long before I ask them to do something.

Chris: Great. And how do you feel about the training event now?

Terry: Better.

Chris: Terry, it is important that you mentally rehearse and repeat the positive imagery two or three times in advance of the training. Every time you reinforce the positive image, you programme your mind for success and confidence. Let your mind brag to yourself how great you could be. Every time you fill your mind with images of the correct actions, you raise your competence, and you raise your confidence. So let mental preparation and rehearsal be an important way to boost your confidence.

Terry: I have read something about mental rehearsal before. Isn't it true that top athletes mentally rehearse their performance before a big game?

Chris: Yes, it is. And even during a big game. So too do top chess players, actors and business leaders. The average person worries about the future and it saps their confidence. The champions rehearse the future and it builds their confidence. So rehearse and mentally prepare your mind for more confidence.

Terry: Thanks, Chris. I will do that.

Four days later I met with Terry after the presentation.

Chris: Hi, Terry. How did your presentation go?

Terry: Good, Chris. Very good. I did a really neat job and got a first-class response from the delegates. In fact, it went almost exactly as I had envisioned it. The whole thing was a real confidence builder.

Chris: Thanks, Terry. That's what I wanted it to be.

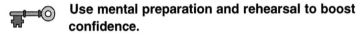 **Use mental preparation and rehearsal to boost confidence.**

Summary of counselling method

Here is a summary of the steps

1. Introduce the session ... then
2. Ask questions that will identify the current situation.
3. Ask questions that will identify their desired situation.
4. Ask questions that will identify the personal resources (knowledge and skills) they will need to acquire.
5. Ask questions that will identify the external resources (money, time, cooperation of others) they need to acquire.
6. Ask questions that will inspire emotions of motivation.
7. Ask questions that will inspire emotions of confidence.

Summary of all the counselling principles from this section

- Purpose is the root of happiness.
- If you want to instill enthusiasm in people, help them to discover an exciting, clear purpose.
- A clear motive creates a potent motivation.
- Have a person realise when he is drifting.
- Help people to overcome unhappiness by showing them how to focus on a personal goal.
- Help people to organise their priorities and encourage them to act in accordance with them.
- Help others to identify and resolve their contradictions.
- Help the people discover a purpose that will allow them to express their full potential.
- Ask people to quantify their goals numerically.
- Connect people to their experience, not their fears.
- Have people talk about the future in affirmative language.
- Be a 'rational optimist'.
- Ask people to set time limits for themselves.
- Encourage others to think logically and base plans on facts not wishes.
- Learn the difference between 'I can't' and 'I don't know how'.
- Tell people that every reasonable desire is possible, provided the person knows what to do
- As a counsellor, and a friend, learn to say this to people: 'You can, if you learn how!'
- Be ready to distinguish between those who lack 'specific contextual experience' and those who lack 'general life experience'.

- Ask people to consider finding a role model.

- Help people to negotiate and arrange their time.

- Keep people in contact with reality, and that includes financial realism.

- Do not let people pretend that the things they need will appear by magic.

- Help people to enlist the cooperation of others in mutually beneficial relationships.

- Learn the pleasure/pain questions and be ready to use them to inspire action in others.

- Build their confidence by building feelings of competence.

- Encourage people to use mental preparation and rehearsal to boost confidence.

Section Four
Coaching

Coaching is a form of directive teaching based on demonstration, explanation, feedback and encouragement

Coaching is distinguished from counselling in that coaching is directive, whereas counselling is non-directive.

Our method of counselling was based on *non-directive questioning*. The key concept was questions.

Our method of coaching is based around the concepts of *demonstration, practice and feedback*. The emphasis is on 'feedback', both 'on-target' and 'off-target' (positive and negative feedback).

Coaching is based on the application of a simple five-part 'Success Formula' that has been known for centuries and has assumed many names. Some people call it 'the learning loop', others call it the 'feedback cycle'.

It is a formula for all successful action and it looks like this.

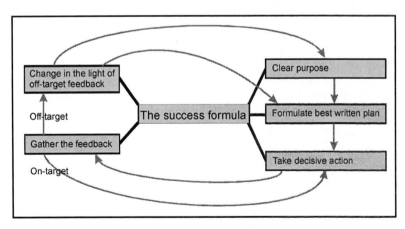

The success formula

The five steps of the success formula are as follows:

Step one: Name a clear purpose
Step two: Formulate your best, written plan
Step three: Take decisive action
Step four: Gather the feedback: both on-target and off-target
Step five: Change in the light of off-target feedback.

 Use the 'success formula' to guide your actions, and the actions of others.

This is a cycle, a process, not a list. You go round it, not down it.

Sometimes I hear people ask, *'When I have got the feedback and made the change, what do I do next?'*

You can guess my answer. *'Check that you still want to achieve the goal, and formulate your next plan.'*

'So, I go round again?'
'Yes, that's right.'
'How many times do I go round?'
'As many times as it takes to achieve the goal.'
What do I do when I achieve the goal?'
'Celebrate, feel good and then ... Set a new goal!'

The success formula is a never-ending process.

As a coach, I want you to understand and use the five-step success formula, and encourage those you are helping to do the same.

It is simple. So simple, I want you to teach it to everyone.

This five-step process is a description of all successful action. You can use it to help others achieve more. It always works, no matter what the time and place and no matter what the context – from baking a cake to writing a book.

Let's take these last two as examples.

Use the success formula to bake a cake:
Step one – name a clear purpose
Imagine that you decide to bake a cake. Before you can begin, you have to know exactly what kind of cake. A coconut cake, a jam

sponge, or what? Before your can do anything else, you must decide exactly what you want. When you are clear on your purpose, you have achieved step one, clarity of purpose (all the points we made earlier about 'purpose' still apply).

Step two – formulate a written plan

You need to have a plan to guide your actions. In the cake scenario, you will have a recipe. A recipe is a written plan of action telling you three things:

1. what resources you will need
2. what actions to take
3. what order to take them.

Having a written plan is important. But why a written plan? Why not a plan you make up in the moment? There are four reasons for developing a written plan.

1 You should have a written plan because a written plan acts as a permanent template, a blue print that you can use to check yourself against.
2 Writing plans forces you to think more specifically and carefully because you have to find the words to express your vision. In finding the words, you are forced to clarify meaning to yourself.
3 A written plan can be checked by others. Other people may see errors or omissions in the plan, that you have missed.
4 A written plan can be distributed to others if necessary, so you can more easily communicate your intentions.

Step three – take decisive action

This is the practical application of the plan, the hands-on practice, the work.

Many people put off the 'doing' part of the success formula. They have goals and they have plans. They have the resources. They just don't do anything with them. The success formula demands action!

Step four – gather the feedback, both on-target and off-target

As you prepare the cake, you should be checking the results of your current actions. Are they in line with achieving the goal or not? Is the mixture smooth or lumpy? Is the taste sweet enough or not?

Not looking for or not noticing the 'feedback result' will cause the 'final result' to be different to what you intend.

 You must give and get feedback.

But feedback comes in two varieties – **on-target and off-target**.

On-target feedback occurs when your current actions result in consequences that are equal to or better than those you anticipated.

The proper response to on-target feedback is,

'Keep doing what you are doing.'

Most people like on-target (positive) feedback. It makes them feel good.

Off-target feedback occurs when your current actions result in consequences that are not what you intended or worse than you want.

The proper response to off-target feedback is two fold,

'Analyse the feedback.'

Then, if you decide the feedback is accurate,

'Change in the light of off-target feedback'.

People do not like off-target (negative) feedback – it makes them feel bad.

As a coach you will need to practice the art of giving both on and off-target feedback in a professional way.

Step Five – change in the light of off-target feedback

Off-target feedback tells you that your current actions are not working, that your actions are not taking you to your goal. The proper response then, is to **change something**.

'Change something' means that you must be prepared to return to step one of the formula, (to check that the goal itself is still valid, and desirable) and continue through the cycle again, re-formulating and altering plans, taking fresh actions and gathering more feedback, varying procedures whenever the feedback tells you that it is necessary.

In this way, you move through the task until you have achieved your outcome; in this case, a beautiful cake.

All successful endeavours follow the same five-step pattern.

Let's take a second example before we look in detail at the model and apply it to coaching others.

Example 2 – Use the success formula to write a book

I used the success formula method to write this book, in the following way:

Step one – know your outcome

I was told the theme of the book that was required, how many words the publisher wanted and by what date.

Step two – formulate a written plan

I worked out a written plan of what ideas I would include, and their place in the book. I planned the book and sent the plan to the publisher for approval.

Step three – take decisive action

I wrote my first draft. That was the 'hard graft'. The doing. The hard work.

Step four – gather the feedback

I had two people read the draft and had them critique the content and style. They gave me some positive feedback together with lots of off-target feedback

Step five – change in the light of off-target feedback

I made changes in the light of the critical feedback, re wrote the book and repeated the success formula process. I continued with the same five steps until James, the publisher, was happy and published the book. [This step is still going on as the original typescript is being edited – Ed]

A good question

You may be wondering – if success is defined by these five simple steps, why doesn't everyone do it? That is a good question!

Here is the answer. The success formula is simple but not easy. It is simple to understand, but not necessarily easy to apply. Why? Because the success formula contains three elements that many people have difficulty with.

1   Many people do not have clear goals.

2 Many people do not take 'critical feedback' very well.

3 Many people do not like to change.

Most people have trouble with these three elements in the following way:

1 Many people are clear about what they do not like. But they are often not clear about what they would replace it with (as we have seen).

2 Many people think that, if their plan does not work out (i.e. if they take action on a plan and the result they get is not what they want), then they have failed (when, in fact, the result should be seen only as 'off-target feedback').

3 Many people want stability, certainty, and no change.

As a coach, understand two things:

1 How the success formula works in practice

2 How to help people overcome the three difficult elements.

The success formula can be conveniently summed up in just five words, like this:

1 Purpose
  2 Plan
    3 Action
      4 Feedback
        5 Change

You could look at 'Coaching' as the application of the success formula to others. Your goal, as the coach, is to help the people you are coaching through the elements of the success formula, step-by-step, round the cycle, as many times as is necessary until they achieve their goal.

The success formula is a universal methodology for successful action and, as such, can be applied to every context. We are going to apply it to the person we are coaching. It will be the basis of their actions as we coach them.

Let us now look at the elements of the success formula and how you might apply it to coaching others. The first step is to achieve clarity of purpose.

Step 1 – Clarity of purpose

As the coach, your first job is to instill sense of 'clarity of purpose' in the mind of other people. They have to have a clear conception of 'the target'. They have to know what they are aiming for, what would constitute success.

For example, my classical guitar teacher, Marguerite, when she is teaching me a new piece, has me listen to a recording of the music. Or she herself will play it for me.

Why does she do that? To give me a vivid idea of exactly what I am trying to achieve. Imagine trying to learn to play a piece of music that you had never heard before. It would be more difficult wouldn't it?

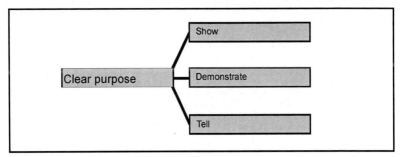

There are three ways you can help other people to achieve the state of 'clarity of purpose'.

1 You could show them an example
2 You could demonstrate it by your own actions
3 You could tell the person, verbally what is required.

Let's look at each one in turn.

Show

The easiest way to achieve clarity is simply to show the person a concrete example of 'the finished product'.

For example, when I teach groups 'minute writing skills' at a London council, I show the group an example of professional, accurate and brief minutes, taken by a previous delegate. That document acts as a 'compass setting' for the rest of the course. Everything we do from then on is guided by it.

We know what we are trying to achieve, and the rest of the day is spent figuring out how to get there and by practicing the techniques.

When an art teacher was trying to teach the rules of perspective, he showed the class a copy of Leonardo da Vinci's working sketches. The sketches showed the geometric lines disappearing to various 'vanishing points'. This acted as a vivid example of all the points the art teacher would present later, and showed immediately to the students, how they might organise their own work.

When an engineering teacher was trying to teach students the rules of thermodynamics, he showed them seven completed, fully worked out examples, before asking them to do one for themselves. This acted to give confidence to the students because they could see the method 'in action' enough times to allow them to see the principles involved. They would later be able to more easily use the same principles to tackle questions on their own.

 Showing people 'the target' is often your first step to helping them succeed.

Demonstrate

The second way to achieve clarity in the mind of the other person is to demonstrate, or role model the correct performance.

Remember that we are, by nature, social learners; we learn easily by mimicking others. Think of how children mimic the actions of the adults around them, by imitation. Copying is natural for most people.

For example, watch a mother cooking a lunch in the kitchen with her young child nearby and you will see how the mother's actions are copied by the infant. As we get older, we do not lose that mimicking ability. We tend to mould ourselves, to some degree, to those around us. We learn both good and bad habits from other people.

Use that fact. Demonstrate the correct method. It is an easy and effective way to inspire and is a vital step to helping others to achieve the clarity they need.

Tell, explain

If you cannot show the person a completed example, and if you are unable to role model as an example, then you should take the necessary time to tell the person, verbally, what is required.

Remember that language introduces a degree of ambiguity, because words only represent reality, so a verbal message can often be misunderstood.

If you are in a position that requires you to verbally describe the outcome, you should make every effort to be exact and specific in your use of language. Too much ambiguity will cause confusion and conflict. Spend as much time as is necessary to get your vision message across.

Which one?

Which one of these methods should you use when coaching another?

There is no one definitive answer. It depends on the context. But, I believe you should think about this step before you start your coaching session.

Are you going to show examples, role model, describe, or some combination? Obviously, you can use all three, but in what order? And what would be the balance between the three?

Think this through before you start the coaching session.

If you do this part well, everything flows. If you do not, everything that follows will be more difficult.

How would you present these?

What method of 'gaining clarity' would you use, and why? Imagine you were planning a coaching session to teach people the following skills.

1 Imagine you wanted to teach an elderly person you know, how to use a new computer. How would you start? Jot down some ideas:

2 Imagine you wanted to teach a person a three-ball juggle.
  How would you start?

3 Imagine you wanted to coach a person on 'lifting heavy
  items'? How would you start?

Step 2 – Formulate a written plan

It is important that you plan ahead, if your goal is to coach others. Spend a few minutes before the coaching session mapping out your approach to the person and the skill or task you are coaching.

Unless you plan, you will be forced to make it up as you go along, which is not the best way to achieve anything. It is important to think about the people you are coaching and their relationship to the material or skills they want to learn.

 Take into account the nature of the learner.

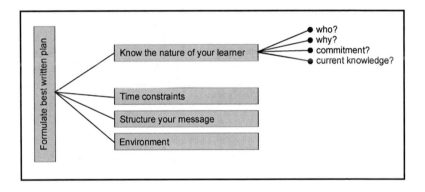

Taking into account the nature of the learners
What aspects of your learners should you take into account?

There are numerous aspects you could take into account, including the following.

Who are your learners?
- Create a picture of your learners in your mind's eye. Ask yourself what style would appeal to them most.
- Meet your learners on their level before you try to change their thinking.

Why are they learning?
- What is the purpose or reasons motivating them to learn?
- If they are not motivated, you must motivate them!

- Trying to coach a de-motivated person is a waste of your time and effort.
- Remember that people are motivated by both pleasure and pain.
- Discover the pleasurable consequences the learner will gain if he learns the material or masters the skill.
- Or, discover the painful consequences the person will avoid, if he masters the material or skill.
- Then, use both these motivators to inspire interest in the session

What is their current level of knowledge?

- How much knowledge do your learners have already? Nobody you are coaching comes to you 'tabula rasa', Blank slate.. They come to you with a certain level of existing knowledge.
- It is important that you have a clear picture of their current knowledge.
- If you assume too much knowledge, you might swamp the learners with material that is too advanced or with a pace that they find overwhelming.
- If you underestimate the person's knowledge, you might waste valuable time or you might come across as patronising.

 Pitch your message to match and then advance their knowledge.

What is their level of commitment?

- Do your pupils *want* to learn your material or do they *have* to learn it?
- If they do not want to learn it, but have to, keep it short, snappy and to the point.

What style is likely to motivate them?

- Everyone has a learning style; some people prefer a very technical approach. Others prefer a looser style. You should develop a feel for the character and learning style of others and adapt yourself to their individual needs.

So, how should you best present your material?

- Having answered the previous questions, you should have a grip on the best approach that will keep your learners' interest.
- Keep this solidly in your mind as you present.

External factors to take into account

There are things other than the learner, to take into account when you are planning a coaching session. There are environmental factors to consider, for example:

How much time?

How much time do you have for this coaching session? If you are short on time, you will not have time to cover everything, so you will have to prioritise. Work out, in advance, what elements of your message are essential, and which ones are details. If you do not work out the relative importance of information, you might waste valuable time.

 Work to a written plan

Structure your message like a tree

To teach knowledge or skills to another, it is important to organise your material. The more complex the material, the more important it is that you consider the structure of your message.

Remember that knowledge is hierarchical. It has a branching structure, like a tree. At the base, are the **'fundamental ideas'** (the trunk of the tree). These are the essential ideas, categories or skills that go to make up the core of the subject.

All subjects have fundamentals: for example, in mathematics it is arithmetic – addition, subtraction, multiplication and division. Without a firm grasp of the fundamentals, subsequent knowledge or the acquisition of new skills is impossible.

Flowing from the fundamentals are the higher-level ideas, or skills. These are called **main themes** (the branches of the tree). For example, flowing from arithmetic there are main themes, such as geometry, trigonometry and algebra.

Beyond these ideas are the minor themes, advanced details and refinements (leaves) that are the very tips of current knowledge or expertise. In mathematics, high iteration fractals, boolean calculus and so on.

As a coach, It is important to work out the proper logical structure of your subject, i.e. the relative importance of each of the ideas, or skills you intend to be coaching.

What would happen to a coach who was not sure of the structure of the topic he was coaching? He wouldn't be able to coach anyone properly – why? Because the learner would not be taken though a logical sequence. As a result, confusion would creep in and progress would stop.

Proper presentation sequence

Let us assume then, that as a good coach, you have worked out a structure. Then it is important to present the material in the proper sequence (fundamentals first, main themes, minor themes and then details).

Some coaches, people who really know their stuff, have the tendency to jump about through their material, hopping from one item to another. They do it because they can. They know their material well enough to flit about without confusing themselves.

But what about the learner? Moving around the intellectual structure upsets the learner, because he does not know the material. And what happens? Again, confusion reigns and progress slows down to a snail's pace.

 Structure your message

Choose the right environment

If you are coaching practical skills, you will need a certain amount of space. For example, if you are teaching people first aid, you will need sufficient space for the practical exercises involved. Insufficient or inappropriate space will disrupt the session and reduce your effectiveness as a coach. So it makes good sense for you to think ahead and ensure that you have the proper space arranged.

Step 3 – Take decisive action

Your learners must take action. They must do something. They must tackle the problem. Practice the skills.

Practice

Assume we have given our learners the clarity of purpose they need, a thorough explanation and demonstration of examples, and we have done some role modelling. Now we hand over the reins to them and encourage them to have a go. Now is the time they put into practice the ideas they have learned.

This is a key moment because there is a big difference between knowing what to do in theory and actually being able to do it in practice.

For example, I am currently studying a method of mental arithmetic called 'the Trachtenburg method'. It is a system that allows the learner to perform addition, subtraction, long multiplication, squares and roots, mentally, without the need to write out the intermediate steps on paper.

The system involves an extended sequence of steps, each one of which is easy to understand, but which means holding in mind intermediate numbers, whilst calculating others. It is fairly easy for me to understand what I should do, but it is another thing for me to actually do it correctly, without errors.

The ability to understand is one thing. The ability to perform is another. And the ability to perform is a function of repetition and practice.

 Repetition is the greatest teacher.

Because the practical element is the time when people find out how they are actually going to measure up, some back away from this part of the Success Formula.

They procrastinate, and put things off..

For example, my daughter Rebecca is learning French. She does not like French because she finds it difficult. She finds it difficult because she does not know sufficient vocabulary to construct full sentences. And because she cannot create sentences, she does not do well in class, which means she dislikes French.

This is a self-reinforcing cycle, isn't it? It looks like this:

- Rebecca does not like doing French, so she ...
- does not study enough, so she ...
- is unable to form sentences, so she ...
- performs badly in class, so she ...
- does not like doing French ... ...

The way to break this cycle is to knuckle down and learn more French vocabulary and grammar. If Rebecca did this, she would form French sentences more easily, and she would do better in class. That would help her to enjoy the lessons, which would make it easier to learn.

This would be a self-perpetuating, positive cycle *comme ceci*:

- Rebecca learns enough, so that she ...
- is able to form sentences in French, so that she ...
- does well in class, so that she ...
- likes French lessons more, so that she ...
- studies more often, so that she ...
- is able to form more complex French sentences ... ...

This is a self-reinforcing **positive** cycle. One that a good coach wants to establish.

So, I obtained a list of the hundred most useful words, those hundred words that make up 50% of spoken language. I explained to Rebecca that if we could we could learn them, together, it would make her French easier and better.

Rebecca agreed that she should, she agreed that she would. But whenever it came to sitting down and actually working, she always found an excuse not to. As a result, there is a still a gap between her actual performance and her potential.

This situation is common and, as a coach you will meet it often.

 Help people beat procrastination

Procrastination – the opposite of taking action

Procrastination is the destructive habit of putting off acting on the things you know you should do. As a coach, you will want to understand procrastination. You will meet it in the people you are coaching. You will need to help them overcome it.

Why do people procrastinate on practising things they know they really should do?

There are two main reasons why people procrastinate.

1   They think that practice will be, in some way, painful
2   They are more attracted by a more pleasurable alternative.

People procrastinate because they think that the practice will be in some way, a painful experience. The pain might take one of a number of forms. For example:

☹   the pain of boredom
☹   the pain of discovering that they are not as skilled as they thought they were
☹   the pain of 'failure'.

Others procrastinate because they're more attracted to a more pleasurable alternative. For example, my partner Linsdey is learning Spanish. She puts off practice because, when faced with the option of reading an exciting novel or reviewing her Spanish verbs, the novel always seems so much more appealing.

As a coach you will need to anticipate the problem of procrastination and develop methods to overcome it. (You can apply the questioning techniques outlined earlier in this book to inspire a feeling of motivation).

As your learners are practising, you are watching and listening closely. Your job here is three fold.

1   Encourage and motivate the learner
2   Identify areas of good performance, and give on-target feedback.
3   Identify areas that need improving and give off-target feedback.

Step 4 – Give people feedback

This next point is very important. Memorise this definition and ponder its significance.

> ## The definition of feedback
>
> Feedback is defined as *'information that identifies and compares the actual results of a particular action, against the desired results for that action.'*
> There are two kinds of feedback - on-target and off-target.

 Learn to give accurate, well-timed, objective and encouraging feedback. It is an essential coaching skill.

There is a knack to giving effective feedback. And all coaches should develop The Knack. We need to talk about both kinds of feedback : on-target and off-target. I want to talk about off-target feedback first, because it is the more difficult to do correctly.

Off-target feedback

First let us review the Success Formula.

1 **Purpose**
  2 **Plan**
    3 **Action**
      4 **Feedback on/off**
        5 **Change in the light of off-target feedback.**

You can see that the success formula has 'off-target feedback' built in. The problem is that most people do not readily accept off-target feedback. They perceive off-target feedback as 'negative feedback', 'criticism', or 'failure'. As a result, they lose heart or become frustrated and angry.

But let me ask you a question. Logically, is it good or bad for people to know when their actions are 'off-target', i.e. not taking them towards their goal?

Of course, it is a good thing to know when your actions are off-target, but often unpleasant to discover it. So, we have to be able to develop an atmosphere where off-target feedback is not seen by our learners as a bad thing, but as a good thing.

The creed of a coach

There is a belief that I want you to adopt. It is related to off-target feedback. It represents the attitude that we want to inspire in our learners. It is this.

> **I no longer see feedback as failure.**
> **Rather, I see it as information I need**
> **to make my next improvement.**

Living by this creed, makes failure almost impossible, because 'failure' simply becomes off-target feedback, to be analysed, evaluated, and utilised to inform the next improvement.

Saying this and understanding it is one thing, living and breathing this philosophy is another. It is something to practice and to teach others on a daily basis.

When applying this concept to others, you may want to bear in mind the following six principles. They are the specific details of how to give effective off-target feedback.

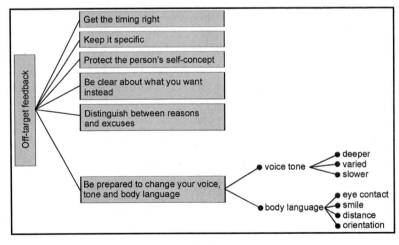

***Effective feedback rule 1* – Get the timing right**

When giving feedback, timing is important. In essentials, the rule for timing is simple.

 Give the feedback as soon after the event as is practical.

Putting the same point negatively, *don't wait too long between the action and the feedback.* People need to know how they are doing. And they need to know it quickly.

If you do not correct a wrong action, it is repeated. After a number of repetitions, it becomes habitual. It is difficult to break a bad habit once it is established.

We need to give our learners accurate feedback quickly, otherwise their errors become automatic and the mistakes solidify into hard-to-break, bad habits.

For example, Can was learning to drive a car. He thought he would save money by having his father, David, teach him. Unfortunately David was not a professional instructor. He was a sales rep, who drove many miles every day, none of them safely.

David had many bad habits that he regarded as 'Advanced knowledge'. For example, David taught Can that 'the best way to position yourself when reversing the car into a parking space is to turn around in your seat, rest your left arm upon the top of the front passenger seat, like this, and steer the car with your right hand only. That way, you can whip the car into the space like a pro!'

Can eagerly learned this method and it soon became a fixed habit. When Can finally went to a professional instructor, he discovered Dad's method was wrong.

But what do you think happened each time Can needed to make a reversing manoeuvre? That's right, his left arm came up automatically. It cost him dearly. Can failed two driving tests and it took three months to retrain Can to the correct method.

Let us take another example.

Imagine you were trying to house train your new pet dog, Patch.

Suppose you leave Patch, at 8.00 am, to go to work. At 9.00, Patch poops on the carpet! You return home at 6.00 pm and find the mess.

You look for Patch. At 6.01 you find him, spank him with a rolled up newspaper and shout 'No! Bad dog!'

Question – what did Patch learn?

Did he learn not to pooh on the carpet, or did he learn something else? He learned to avoid his coach. He learned literally nothing about being house trained, did he? Why?

One reason was that the timing was wrong. The delay between the action and the feedback was too long. To be effective, the feedback has to be immediate. Both these examples tell us the same thing:

 When coaching, give immediate feedback whenever possible.

 Effective feedback rule 2: **Keep it specific to particular quality standards. Do not generalise.**

The next coaching skill for you to perfect is the ability to verbalise a specific feedback message. Make sure that you can name the **exact behaviour** you want to give feedback on.

Tell the learner exactly what the error was, in behavioural terms, and immediately name the correct behaviour. Do not allow any verbal ambiguity to creep into your language.

Let me give you some contrasting examples of language so that you can readily see the difference between proper coaching language, i.e. specific clear and objective, and poor feedback language which is vague, unclear and subjective.

Suppose the situation is that I am coaching someone to lift heavy objects safely. Compare these feedback statements. The first example in each pair is badly worded; the second example in each pair is objective and specific. Look at the examples and see the difference.

✗   Steve, you re doing that wrong. You're too sloppy. Be firmer in your approach.

✓   Steve, you have your legs too straight and you are bending your back too much. Instead, bend your knees more and keep your spine straighter.

✘   Don't plonk it down. You'll do yourself a mischief.

✓   As you lower the box, keep the weight as near to your body as possible and lower it slowly to the floor.

✘   Always take a professional approach to lifting heavy objects. If you mess about you will injure your back .

✓   Keep your mind focused only on the job at hand. Head, up, back straight, legs bent, and put the load onto the thighs, not the lower back.

Here is a second example. Imagine the situation is that you are teaching the person telephone sales skills. Read these feedback statements. The first example in each pair is poorly worded because it is too vague or emotional; the second example in each pair is better, because it is more specific and clear.

✘   No. You didn't introduce yourself properly. You came across as too pushy.

✓   When the person answers the phone, remember to introduce yourself by saying something like 'Hello, my name is Jason, and I am calling you from High Society Products, London.'

✘   You messed that up. You didn't ask for the appointment.

✓   Next time you call; ask the person if they have their dairy handy. When they say yes, ask them 'I would like to come and see you in person. What date would be best for you?'

✘   When you get a rejection, don't worry about it. Just soldier on and try to do better next time.

✓   Remember that Telephone Sales is a numbers game. Statistically, you can expect nine people to say 'no', for every one that says 'yes'. And you can expect five appointments to earn one sale. So expect a high ratio of 'nos' and move on.

Notice how the first example in each pair is more likely to create a negative reaction.

The second example in each pair is more likely to create a thoughtful, and therefore more positive reaction.

So, the message is clear:

When correcting another person use, defined, specific, objective language.

 Effective feedback rule 3 – **Protect the person's self-concept**

The 'self-concept' is one of the most important discoveries you can make in your study of people. Psychologists tell us that people always act in accordance with their own self-concept.

If a person has a good self-concept, he or she has good relationships, they are productive and happy.

To the degree that a person has a poor or damaged self-concept, that person has fraught relationships, is unhappy and unproductive.

Self-concept is defined as:

The mental sum of the thoughts and beliefs that a person has about his or her own character, abilities and potential.

The self-concept is one of the keys to unlocking better performance. So as a good coach, always protect their self-concept. Even better ...

 Work to build up the self-concept of others.

Make others feel stronger. There are two ways to do that:

1 Whenever criticising another, use objective, non-evaluative language (as we have already discussed).
2 Whenever the person does anything good, use the opposite language pattern. Whenever a person does a good action, use evaluative and emotional language to build the persons self-image. Praise and build up the self-concept. Each time the person does something positive, use the positive behaviour to reinforce the good self-concept.

If the behaviour is good, make the **link between the self-concept and the behaviour.**

For example, imagine I was John's coach. He has written a report and he has done a very good job. I could use that fact to boost his self-image. Because my evaluation of his work is good, I should include evaluative language in the feedback.

'John, That report you wrote yesterday on the Diamond project was excellent. It was persuasive and well set out. You did a great job. Well done.'

But if the person does something wrong, do not use the behaviour to attack the self-concept. Instead make no link between the self-concept and the behaviour. Because my evaluation of the person's work is bad, you should exclude evaluative language in the feedback.

 Do not use evaluative language when criticising
Do use evaluative language when praising.

So, if the diamond report had been badly written, I would not link the action to the self-image. I would remain objective:

'John, the Diamond Project report you wrote yesterday had four spelling errors and at least three factual errors. The pricing was wrong. The layout was a straight copy from last years report.

Please would you look at it again and correct the points I have mentioned. Thanks.'

This idea of the self-concept does not mean that you should not judge others, or that you should have no negative feelings associated with others. I believe that is natural and proper to judge behaviour as right and wrong, good or bad. And I know that other people's behaviour might trigger some bad feelings in your soul.

My point here is not that we should be unemotional, but rather we should be careful in the way we use language to express our meaning.

For example, imagine that I leave an electric cooker on and another person is burned as a result. Imagine that, when you find out what I did, you call me in. You say, *'Chris, that was stupid!'*

If you said that, you would be using my negative behaviour as the excuse to launch an attack on my self-concept.

Under those circumstances, one of two things may happen. And they are both bad.

1 When I hear you call me stupid, in my soul, I agree with you.

I may think to myself, *'All my life people have called me stupid. My mum called me stupid. My dad called me stupid. So did the teachers at school. I am a failure!'*

In other words, I accept your negative 'label'. If that happens, what can you say about my self-concept? Has it got weaker or stronger? Weaker, of course..

So, what about my ability to tap into my potential ? Has that ability improved, or worsened? Obviously, I am worse off.

2   The second possibility when you call me 'stupid' is that I disagree with you. The vast majority of people will fight an attack on their self-concept. They must preserve the integrity of their self-image. It is a psychological human need to preserve the self-concept, in order to keep a certain level of self-esteem.

So, even if I accept I was wrong to leave the electric ring on, I would not accept the label of 'stupid'. To do so is too painful to my ego.

I will fight you. I will find excuses to justify myself, or I will become defensive or even aggressive towards you.

Remember the issue here is not whether the negative judgement is 'right or wrong'. The issue is whether it is an effective communication style to verbalise the negative judgement.

It serves no purpose for you to attack my self-concept. Instead you should be protecting my self-image, whilst you go about changing my behaviour.

 Remember – preserve and build up people's self-concept.

 Effective Feedback Rule 4 **– Be specific about what you expect instead.**

It is not enough to know what you do not want from others. You should also know what you *do want.*

Telling a person *what not to do* is not enough. Telling a person *why a thing is not right* is not enough.

In addition, we *must know what we do want.* So think before you speak and ask yourself, 'What do I want this person to do instead of what he or she is doing now?'

In other words, you must offer the person a way out, a way forward, from the current position.

If your coaching style is based on negation, that is telling people what not to do, the result will be frustration and confusion. It is important to tell people where they are going wrong, but the emphasis should always be on the affirmative, on the *right next move*. If your coaching style is founded on the affirmative, positive, right actions, the result will be clarity, motivation and goal focus.

 ### *Effective Feedback Rule 5* – Distinguish between reasons and excuses.

Is there a difference between a 'reason' and an 'excuse' for not doing something? You bet there is a difference! A reason is true, logical, undeniable and unavoidable. An excuse is none of these, i.e. an excuse is untrue, illogical, dishonest or avoidable.

Imagine you give a person some off-target feedback, and ask him to make a change in behaviour. Imagine that he does not make the change. You will want to ask, 'why not?'

Here is the point: When you ask the question and that person answers, listen very closely. You have to classify their answer into one of two categories, either:

- the **reason** they cannot change, or
- the **excuse** they use to avoid changing.

When you listen to others, do you consciously distinguish between reasons and excuses? It is important that you do, because, as a coach you will need to have a different policy for each.

What would happen to the coach who does not distinguish between reasons and excuses, i.e. one who is willing to accept anything as a 'reason'? Such a coach would be ineffective. He would be unable to sustain progress in another person. The other person would be able to conjure up any plausible but false excuse and evade the actions necessary for continued progress.

So as a good coach, learn to distinguish between excuses and reasons and then act accordingly.

Question – who should decide *for you* what constitutes a reason and what is an excuse in any particular case?

Write your answer here.

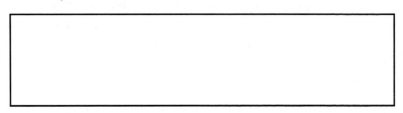

I hope that you have written that you make that decision for yourself. Nobody else can.

It takes a certain degree of courage to stand in front of somebody and make the decision that you are not going to accept their excuse.

Many people do not want to make that decision.

For example, on a training course I was presenting last year, I was asked by a delegate called Wayne, *'Chris, who am I to judge? I cannot be 100% sure that my judgement will be correct. I may get it wrong: I may either believe someone who is giving me an excuse, or disbelieve someone who is telling me the truth. I don't want to take the risk'*

I said, *'Wayne, I understand that you may make a mistake. So I would advice that, if there doubt, give the benefit of that doubt to the other person.*

But that does not mean that you can completely evade the responsibility of making the decision. If you want to coach others, there will be times when the other person does not follow through and does not do the right things.

There will be times when the other will try to fob you off with excuses. What kind of coach would you be if you accepted anything as true?

Let me give an example. If I was your coach, and I accepted any excuse you gave me, how mush respect would you have for me?'

The delegate said, *'Not much. But how can I ensure that my judgement will be correct all the time?'*

'You cannot ensure that your judgement will right 100% of the time. And It does not have to be. Correct most *of the time will suffice'.*

Your policy towards reasons and excuses should be different.

If you think the person is giving good *reasons*, then you should **negotiate** a good compromise solution. There is no sanction.

If you think you are hearing unreasonable excuses, do not negotiate. Do not negotiate with a person who offers only excuses.

 Earn a reputation for being a person who responds only to reason.

I have another question for you. What would happen to progress if anyone could invent any excuse to avoid doing something, and as a result, gain a concession?

Progress would stop. If people can evade effort and replace it with an excuse, then inevitably some will. But progress is based on intelligent efforts, not intelligent excuses. So as coaches, we need to have high standards and a high degree of awareness towards distinguishing reasons from excuses.

 Effective feedback rule 6 **– Be prepared to change your body language according to the character of the other person.**

Human communication is through three channels. They are:

- words (verbal language)
- voice tonality (pitch, range, intonation, volume, etc.)
- body language (posture, eye contact, gestures, etc).

We have been talking about 'what to say' to the other person- the language component of your communication. Getting the words right is important. Equally important is your style. How you say it.

The 'how you say it' is governed by your tone of voice and your body language. Let us discuss voice tone and body language, one at a time.

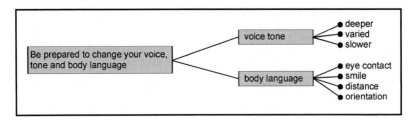

Voice tone

Voice tone relates to the musical aspects of your voice – it pertains to pitch, volume, rate, and emphasis. People respond instinctively to voice tone, either positively or negatively.

There are certain people who have a warm, attractive welcoming voice quality. Their voice tone has a positive effect on others. One of the best examples of a person with a good voice tone, in my opinion, was the actor Richard Burton. I once heard him on the radio, reading names and addresses from the phone book. When he did it, it sounded entertaining.

There are others, who have a flat, monotone droning quality to their voice. They have a negative effect on others. Their voice quality switches off the mind of the listener.

Let us investigate some of the qualities that make the difference between good voice and not-so-good voice.

Here is a summary grid. Look at the grid below and we will go through it step by step.

Good voice tone	Poor voice tone
Deeper	Higher
More Varied	Unvaried- monotone
Slower	Faster

Good voice tone
Speak with a deeper tone. How does a deeper voice affect the listener? Research done by American psychologists proves that people make instinctive judgements of others based upon the tone of the voice of the speaker. Specifically, people judge those with deeper voices as having more authority.

This is thought to be a 'throw back' to an earlier time where status was based upon physical power and strength. Heavier, physically bigger people have deeper voices than smaller people. And bigger people were dominant, so deep voices were associated to higher status. And to a lesser degree, they still are. So a deeper voice lends more authority.

Does this mean you should speak with a fake deep voice? No. Everyone has a voice range. The advice is:

 To improve the impact of your message, use the lower end of your voice range.

Let's look at the opposite. When you hear a high-pitched or shrill voice, what is your emotional reaction? A high-pitched or shrill voice tends to have a negative effect on the mind of the listener. Generally, the person with the shrill voice is perceived to lack authority, and the tone can be irritating.

Variety of tone

A varied tone rises and falls, and emphasises key words and phrases. A monotone voice has little variety, it stays at the same pitch and there is a lack of stress variation.

It is important to vary your voice tone, as opposed to being monotone. When you vary your tone, you inject life and energy into your message. Emotions like enthusiasm, humour and excitement are conveyed by the tone of your voice.

Think of people you regard as a Master Communicators. Is it true that these people have a certain energy and dynamism in the way they use their voice? Think of the opposite. Do you know someone who has a flat, monotone, lifeless voice? When you hear that kind of voice, what effect does it have on your ability to focus on the content?

If a person has a flat, monotone voice, it has a negative effect on the communication.

So the message is clear – vary your voice tone.

Speak Slower

It is important to slow down, when giving a coaching or counselling session. If a person speaks slower, it has a number of positive effects on the communication.

1   It gives the person listening enough time to 'digest' the message. This is important because there is a distinction to be made between 'hearing' and 'understanding'. Hearing is simply the automatic functioning of the ears. Hearing does not take effort.

Understanding is the act of focusing the mind on the *meaning* of what is heard. That is not automatic. It takes an effort of will to focus the mind on the meaning and to make it clear and distinct.

If you speak too fast, the person will hear you, but will not understand.

 Give enough time for your message to 'sink in' before delivering the next one.

2   When you, the coach, slow down, you have more time to select the right words and phrases to express your meaning exactly.

As a consequence of this, people who speak slightly slower are perceived by the listener to be more thoughtful, 'deeper'. Those who speak more quickly are perceived to be more confusing and 'lightweight'.

This is because, if you slow down, the implied message is that you are thinking before you speak. It implies that you are weighing up the evidence and giving careful consideration to your message. So, the person who pauses, and speaks at a slower pace tends to be perceived as more intelligent. The message carries more weight.

For example, next time you have the opportunity, notice how slowly Prime Minister Tony Blair speaks during conferences. He has slowed down markedly over the last few years. Was that accidental? No it was a conscious technique designed to make his message more weighty and considered.

So, again, the point is clear.

 During a coaching session, slow down

Body language

Body language is the other aspect of the non-verbal communication I would like to discuss with you.

Focus some of your attention on developing key aspects of your body language. As a coach you may want to think about the following body language issues:

Your use of:

- eye contact
  - facial expression
    - touch
      - proximity
        - orientation

Let us talk about each one in turn

Eye contact

Eye contact is an important aspect of your non-verbal communication. In my opinion, there has been a lot of contradictory advice given by various authorities on this topic. Over the years I have heard opposite messages:

I have heard one trainer tell me, *'Chris, don't give too much eye contact. It can come across as intimidating and will upset your listener. Instead, keep eye contact down to a minimum both in terms of intensity and frequency.'*

On other occasions I have heard the opposite advice, like this, *'Chris, it is important that you give plenty of positive, direct eye contact. It demonstrates that you are engaged with your listener. If somebody is not giving you eye contact, it is a sure sign they are not listening!'*

Confusing isn't it? As far as I can tell, this is the truth – in relation to eye contact, there are no hard and fast rules that hold true for everyone.

Some people do not like to receive, or give huge amounts of eye contact. I am one of them. If you are explaining something complex to me, and I really want to listen, I will not look at you. I find looking and listening too much. Looking at you, holding your gaze, is a distraction to my listening. If I really need to listen, I can't look. Often I will keep my eyes tightly closed so I can better focus on what you are saying.

I know that I am in the minority on this, but I am a member of a sizable minority. There are many people like me. In order to listen, and concentrate, they avoid direct eye contact.

Other people do want direct eye contact. Looking at the other person as they listen allows them to gather additional (non verbal) information. It helps to focus the mind on the message and engages the listener on the speaker.

To these people, not looking would be a sign of dis-interest. Closing the eyes would be a sign of boredom. It may even constitute an insult.

So what should we advice the aspiring coach?

Here is the advice:

 Give approximately the same degree of eye contact that you receive from the other person.

Putting the same advice in another way, don't expect other people to respond the same way you do, but rather let them set the body language pace.

For example, if you were coaching me, you would see that I am not looking at you as you explain things to me. I may even close my eyes tight. Don't worry. Just accept it. That is the way I am. Do not think I am dis-interested because the opposite its true. It is because I am interested that I have my eyes closed.

Notice this fact and don't glare. Ease off on your eye contact and focus on your verbal explanation.

On the other hand, if I was coaching someone who looked directly at me as I spoke, I must recognise that this is a person who needs the visual cues to make more sense of what they are hearing. I should match their eye contact as I speak to them. This will improve the communication between us. I should not avoid their gaze. I should go with the flow and accept their needs as the standard. Simple.

Facial expression – smile often

Manage your facial expressions, because people pay special attention to faces. Your face included.

Facial expression is the most important element of non-verbal communication. And the most important element of facial expression is The Smile.

What does a smile convey? A smile conveys that you, the coach, are pleased to see me. A smile conveys that you are warm and friendly. A smile causes people to relax, which will improve the learning atmosphere. A smile causes a rise in the confidence of those who see it. And a rise in confidence creates improved chances of coaching success.

Another advantage of smiling is that it is easy to practice. If you decided to, you could train yourself to smile more frequently.

Everyone knows how to smile, but some do it more frequently and more genuinely than others. You know a person who does not smile often, don't you?

Picture that person's face. What effect does a glum face have on those around them? Is it positive or negative?

Negative.

So, I have an assignment for you. If you do this assignment you will feel and see the benefits immediately. The assignment is:

 Smile at people more often.

Smile whenever it is appropriate. Smile easily and often. As you smile, catch their eye. Become easier to be with.

Putting the same point negatively – do not be difficult to be with, don't be sombre.

A person who fails to smile appears to be 'cold and distant'. A person who does not smile fails to inspire confidence and motivation. As a result, the atmosphere changes for the worse and your chances of success as a coach are reduced.

But please note, 'Smile more often' means just that; 'more often', not 'non-stop'. Non-stop grinning will seem mindless. And that usually does not help.

If you want to be a successful coach, then you will need to create positive emotional responses in others. So consider improving your smile.

Why not take these steps?

- Notice how frequently you smile at people now.
- Commit to smile at others more easily and frequently.
- Do it for a week.
- Notice the positive results you get.
- Then, do it even more.

Smile more and reap the benefits

Distance

How else can you manage your body language so as to maximise your chances of being a successful coach?

One way to maximise your chances is to become aware of distance. The physical distance that you create between yourself and others is an influential element of your body language. Most people never consider it, but we will.

There are some people who keep their distance, not only metaphorically, but also literally. They do not easily make contact with others.

There are some people who do come across as friendly and warm. They have a good handshake and may lightly guide you with a light touch on your arm.

Distance is a major element in successful non-verbal communication. If you manage 'distance' correctly then it will pay you back with improved levels of rapport and connection.

If you mis-manage this aspect you can come across either as too cold, if you keep your distance, or too intrusive, if you crowd in close.

What are the dos and don'ts of managing interpersonal distance?

Here are some dos to bear in mind:

- Do shake hands with people if appropriate.
- Do sit as close as is reasonable to the person you are coaching.
- Do consider sitting next to the person you are coaching.
- Do consider touching people briefly (one or two seconds) (on the arms only) in order to build rapport.

Here are the 'do nots':

- Do not completely avoid physical touch. You may come across as cold.

- Do not sit or stand too far away from others.
- Do not touch people on any place other than the arms. Avoid putting your hand on people's backs (as politicians are trained to do to 'demonstrate their authority'). Do not touch a person's knees or put your arms around their shoulders.
- Do not sit or stand directly opposite the person you are coaching. Direct, face-to-face positioning can create a confrontational mood, (see below).

Manage your orientation

Orientation is the angle that exists between yourself and the person you are communication with. The angle is there whether you are standing or seated. The angle between you represents a powerful aspect of the unspoken communication that passes between you.

It is a surprising fact that people are emotionally sensitive to small, seemingly insignificant changes in body language factors. These factors include body orientation.

If you do not get the angle right, the atmosphere can be confrontational and ill-tempered. If you think it through and arrange things properly, you can transform the atmosphere and make it welcoming, friendly and productive.

So, how should you organise the seating during a coaching session?

To create a warm, productive atmosphere arrange things so that you are either sitting next to the person you are coaching, or you are sitting at a 90 degree angle, as when sitting at the edges of cornered table.

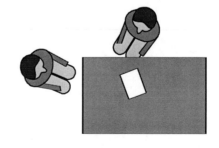

Above all, avoid sitting or standing square-opposite the delegate, face to face. For example, facing across a table. This is a confrontational position that creates tension.

Think about it this way. Imagine you were looking at a conflict situation developing between two people in a bar. As the conflict deepens and tempers fray, you will see the angle of the protagonists change. As the temperature rises, they begin to square up to each other. Literally, that means they change their mutual orientation from the normal angle of about 45 degrees, to an angle 180 degrees opposite each other. Face to face.

This 'opposition stance' is a tension-forming position – it signals high emotion, either sexual attraction, or aggression. Neither of which we want to inspire in a professional coaching session.

So set things up to avoid this position. Instead, sit next to the person. If you sit alongside the people you are coaching, you are metaphorically and literally 'on the same side'. You come across as an ally. You are a friend. As the coach, that is a good place for you to be.

However for some people, being seated next to another person they do not know well may feel too intimate. If you think that is the case, then the best option for you is to sit along the second edge of the table, so that you are at 90 degrees.

You can see this as the intermediary position: the middle ground, friendly but not over friendly; professionally warm, but not intimate.

This may be the position that suits your character best. Or it might be the way you think your delegates may prefer until they get to know you better.

When working with people you do not know well, orientation and seating can make or break the atmosphere.

I am sure you have been put off certain people in the past because they either invaded your space or were too distant, and you thought them aloof.

Don't allow yourself to make the same mistake they did.

Manage your orientation.

So let us summarise the key points to giving off-target feedback.

- **Critical feedback is not failure, it is vital information.**
- **Get the timing right – do it soon.**
- **Keep the feedback to specific standards.**
- **Protect the person's self-concept.**
- **Be specific about what you want instead.**
- **Distinguish between reasons and excuses.**
- **Be prepared to vary your body language and voice tone.**

Give on-target feedback

On-target feedback is telling people that their actions are 'good' and will result in achieving the desired outcome. It is vital that you give plenty of positive, on target feedback immediately you see the person doing anything right. Every time you give somebody positive feedback, in the form of praise, you are raising the chances of success.

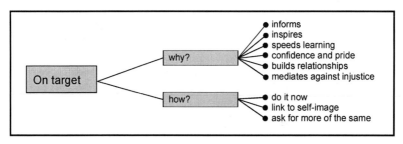

Positive feedback has many encouraging effects on the listener including:

1. informing the person of progress
2. inspiring the person to persevere
3. reinforcing the learning
4. building confidence and pride
5. building a good relationship with the coach.

Let us talk about each of these effects.

Informing the person of his or her progress

When people learn a new skill, they may stumble upon a correct action, almost by chance. They may not necessarily know that what they just did was 'good'.

If they are not immediately told that the action was a correct one, they will have no reason to note it mentally, and will be less likely to repeat it or recall it later. If people are told that their action is 'on track', then they immediately remember it. And they will be more likely to repeat it when required.

For example, I was once watching a trainee carpenter named Paul, sawing a piece of wood in two. He noticed that if he tried to saw all the way through a plank of wood from top edge to bottom edge, as he reached the final millimetres, the wood's weight would cause it to snap, leaving an uneven splintered surface on the underside. So Paul tried a new approach.

He sawed three quarters of the way down, from top edge. Then he stopped and undid the vice, turned the wood over. He then cut again from the new top face to meet the first cut in the middle. The result was a much cleaner finish.

When Paul's coach, Ray, saw this, he immediately said, *'Fantastic idea, Paul. By turning the wood over you eliminate the risk of splintering the visible surface. Excellent. Well done.'*

Paul smiled and pulled his shoulders back. It was clear this message had stuck.

Positive feedback inspires the person to persevere

Giving positive feedback inspires people to persevere. It provides the 'little wins' necessary to keep the motivation high enough to continue even when progress is slow.

Without positive feedback, the learner would have to wait for the achievement of the goal 'in full' before they are emotionally rewarded for their efforts. If the task is a big one, like say, learning a language, then the person may not persevere long enough to make the progress necessary.

With positive feedback, you praise every small achievement. That

182

represents an 'emotional win' and progress is made as a series of 'baby steps'.

Remember too, that many activities and subjects can never be completely 'finished'. There is no point at which the learner can say 'I've finished' and receive their emotional pay off. Examples are learning a musical instrument, fitness training, mathematics or artistic expression.

In many areas of development there is always 'more to do'. There is never a final destination, only a continuous effort. In these cases, there can never be a finishing line or trophy to act as a motivator. In these cases, the motivation comes from regular positive feedback every time a baby step forward is taken.

For example, last year, Linda started studying Spanish because her partner Miguel is from Mexico. She began to make slow progress but when she looked at all the things she did not know, she sometimes felt overwhelmed and disheartened.

She occasionally said to herself, *'I'll never do this!'*

This reaction began to de-motivate Linda and she slowed down her studies. She began to study less, so she made less progress. She even forgot some of the things she thought she knew. This caused her to make even more mistakes which caused her to say to herself again 'I'll never do this!'

Can you see that Linda was in danger of dropping out?

What was the solution to this problem?

Positive feedback. I spoke to Miguel and reminded him of the importance of positive feedback. I told him that he should notice every time Linda made any attempt to speak Spanish. He should offer praise, even if it was only one word – 'Good'.

I said to Miguel, *'Any little bit of progress Linda makes, Miguel, you should "pay her" by noticing the improvement and commenting on it, with a little praise, for what she has done, and a request for more of the same.'*

Miguel agreed that he would, because it was important to him that Linda shares his mother tongue.

Miguel was conscientious. He did exactly as I asked. The following morning when Linda gave Miguel a bowl of cornflakes, Miguel said, *'Gracias, Linda.'*

Linda said quietly, *'De nada.'* ('You're welcome' in Spanish).

Miguel saw his opportunity to give some feedback and took it. He said, *'Excellente! Well done Linda. Give me more. Mas por favor!'*

Linda smiled broadly and said, *'Muchas gracias, senor!'*

Miguel stuck to his task of giving positive feedback each time Linda attempted to express herself in Spanish. As a result, Linda began to speak Spanish more often.

In the evening, Miguel saw Linda reading a book called *Spanish Made Easy*. The praise that Miguel was giving was helping Linda to feel more motivated. And because she felt motivated, she studied and spoke more frequently. So she made more progress.

Miguel praised her more frequently, which inspired Linda to even greater progress. Can you see how important Miguel's commitment to feedback was?

Why not commit to giving positive feedback to the people you coach?

Remember:

Positive feedback feeds the soul.

Positive feedback speeds and reinforces the learning

Positive feedback helps people to learn faster. Learning is often a process of linking actions to results. Here are three simple principles from behavioural psychology that you should learn.

---

1. When people take an action that achieves a pleasurable result, they remember it and repeat that action.

2. When people take an action that achieves a painful result, they remember it and avoid that action.

3. And when people take an action that achieves no result - that is, nothing happens - they forget the action and move on.

In behavioural psychology, this process is called 'conditioning'. As a coach, you want to do everything you can to assist the person to remember and repeat successful actions. So mete out praise, every time your delegate does something right.

It is important that you 'reinforce' and 'condition' every positive action with a pleasurable feedback message (praise).

Let me give you a perfect example.

I was asked to help a mother called Jeannette and her little girl, Stephanie, who was six years old. Jeannette was worried when she discovered that Stephanie was unable to do 'simple subtraction of two digit numbers' at school.

At 6 o'clock one Wednesday evening I visited the house and Jeannette told me, *'Chris, if Steph falls behind in maths class and does not understand the basics, when the others move on to more complex things, poor Steph will be lost.*

I tried to help her with her homework last night but it was impossible – she did not have a clue. She didn't understand the question, let alone the answer.'

I knew Stephanie to be a bright and intelligent girl and I was confident that she had the innate ability. I reasoned that she did not understand the method of subtraction, because she could not 'see it in her mind's eye'.

I thought that, to a six year old, the numbers on the page were simply too abstract for her to relate to and understand what was being asked. So, I decided to bring it back to perceptual reality, a tangible reality, by using beads. I wanted to show Stephanie what the numbers were supposed to be representing.

I put six drinking glasses on the kitchen table, in front of Stephanie. I counted out ten beads for each of the glasses and said to Stephanie, *'Steph. Inside each of these glasses are ten beads. Here is one glass of ten. Here is a second glass of ten.*

If I put these two glasses there, and put three extra beads loose on the table here, how many beads are there all together?'

She looked carefully and thought for a while. Finally she said, *'Twenty and three more.'*

I said, *'Good girl. Excellent!'*

Stephanie smiled.

I said, *'Steph, people normally don't say "twenty and three more", do they? How do they normally say that number?'*

Steph thought for a few seconds and said timidly, *'Twenty three?'*

I said, *'Excellent! SO GOOD, Steph! Write that down here on this paper.'*

She did. I said, *'Very good. Now. If I take one glass of ten and one of the extra beads, and put them way over here, tell me by looking, how many have I taken away from the twenty three?'*

Steph said, *'One glass and one more.'*

I said, *'Very good. How many beads is that added all together?'*

Steph replied, *'Eleven?'*

'REALLY good Steph!' Stephanie clapped her hands together and smiled at me.

I said, *'So can you write 11, underneath the twenty three?'* She did.

I continued, *'Now. Look at the beads we have left. Tell me how many you see, Steph.'*

She said, *'I see a glass and two on the table.'*

'That is exactly right, Steph. Good girl. Now how many beads are there in the glass?'

'Ten.'

'Good. That is right again. And how many are on the table?'

'Two.'

'That's good. So how many all together?

'Twelve.'

'Well done Steph. Twelve. Now can you write the 'twelve' number under the others? Good girl.'

When she had done this, I asked, *'Look at the three different numbers, Steph. What do the numbers mean?'*

Steph's brow furrowed as she looked at the page.

After a long pause she said, *'Twenty three take away eleven beads means there is only twelve left; one glass and two on the table.'*

'Wow! Stephanie. That is exactly right. Show Mum what you can do!'

Stephanie 'explained' it all to her mother, who was fascinated.

When she had finished teaching her mum, Steph said to me, *'More!'*

Now, grab a pen and answer these questions:

How important was it that I gave Steph the positive feedback at the end of every step of the process?

What effect did the feedback have on Steph?

How do you think the session would have gone without the positive feedback?'

The feedback rewarded Stephanie for every step of the process. It 'paid her' immediately for her mental efforts and made her learning easier and faster.

Without the feedback, each step would have seemed like 'effort for no reward' and her mind would have switched off.

No praise = no interest
No interest = no learning
Therefore, no praise = no learning

Remember:

Positive feedback speeds learning

Positive feedback builds confidence and pride

People who feel good about themselves perform better than those who feel bad about themselves, in any situation. It's just the way humans are built.

So, as a coach, one of your goals is to build a strong, confidant 'self-image' in the minds of others. The self-image, you remember, is a mental sum of the thoughts and feelings a person has about their own potential, abilities and character.

People work according to their self-image. A confident self-image improves learning and performance. A depressed self-image hinders learning and performance.

- To the degree that you help others to think positively about their own potential and abilities, is the degree to which you are helping others to achieve their goals. *You are a good coach.*

- And to the degree that you fail to help others to think positively about their own abilities and character, is the degree to which you are preventing others from realising their potential. *You are **not** a good coach.*

Your goal then, is to inspire a productive self-image in the minds of others. And the way to do that is through giving positive feedback. Positive feedback builds the self-image because it is evidence to people that they are 'good', in the sense of being 'efficacious'.

Every time you give positive feedback, you are proving to the people's sub-conscious mind that they are 'winning', and therefore are 'winners'. People then move to a realisation that they are capable, effective and efficient.

That causes them to feel the emotions of pride and self-confidence.

When people have a sense of confidence and pride, based upon a series of achievements, they are in a state that allows them to tap into their personal resources of intelligence and creativity more effectively.

This raises their chances of taking another successful action, which is your trigger to provide more positive feedback … which reinforces the confidence … which improves performance … which creates better results … which creates more positive feedback … and so on.

You get the message, don't you?

You are creating a positive cycle. And it starts with your decision to give more positive feedback.

May I give you a personal example of how positive feedback affected me?

In 1996, I had my first ever opportunity to present myself as a management trainer. My boss, Stewart Harris, asked me to present a two-day course to a group of sales people from a company from Sheffield. There were twenty-three people attending the course.

None of them knew that this was my first attempt at presenting a full corporate training event. Up till that point in time, I had presented two- and three-hour sessions. This was different – two full days!

This was definitely beyond my 'comfort zone'.

I was not 100% sure of my abilities. I knew that I knew the material. I knew what I wanted to say, but I was unsure if I would be able to hold their attention from 9.00am – 5.00pm for two consecutive days.

I prepared myself meticulously before the event. I had my material down pat. Come the day, I was nervous, but in a positive, excited way. My legs were shaking in my trousers as I watched the delegates file in on the Monday morning.

I started well and the delegates responded with enthusiasm. This positive feedback encouraged me, and my self-confidence grew enough to allow me to relax and express myself more fluently.

This made me more effective ... which inspired the delegates more. Their positive response fed my confidence and I continued the rest of the course in the same relaxed way.

At the end of the course, the delegates were asked to fill in a 'feedback form'. When I received the stack of feedback forms, I was relieved and pleased to find they were all positive.

This early success made all the difference because my brain said, *'See? You CAN do it!'*

And later my boss, Stewart, said, *'Chris, you did a great job last week. Keep it up.'*

My confidence and self-esteem were strengthened and I went into my next training day with an improved attitude based on positive feedback.

So please remember:

Positive feedback builds confidence

Praise and positive feedback builds good relationships

As a coach, you need to be good at building effective relationships with other people. So you should use plenty of positive feedback and praise.

People want to be around those who make them feel good about themselves. Positive feedback causes people to smile inside and feel stronger. So people want to be around those who give positive feedback.

The message is this:

If you give positive feedback, you will attract and motivate others.

If you don't, you won't.

Let's look at the same point from the opposite direction. People do not like managers and coaches who only give destructive criticism, or those who fail to appreciate their efforts. As a coach, you want to build links and bridges between your mind and that of your people. So do not fall into the trap of omitting praise.

Let me ask you a question. At work, have you ever heard people say, *'I hear soon enough from my boss whenever things go wrong, but I never get any praise when things go right'*?

As I go from business to business presenting training to managers and leaders, I hear this sentiment expressed by the delegates.

What effect does this reaction have on the relationships between the managers and the others? Does it help or hinder?

Let me ask you another question. Have you ever worked hard to complete a task to a high standard within a short deadline, achieved a good result, and then NOT heard one word of appreciation from your boss?

When that happens, what is the effect on your level of motivation and commitment? Do you feel more or less motivated? Clearly, you will feel less motivated. Why? Because failure to get positive feedback feels like an injustice.

Giving positive feedback represents giving people what they need and deserve, both intellectually (to improve their learning) and socially (to build a sense of pride). You can build positive bonds by letting people know how well they are doing.

On-target feedback mediates against the effects of 'organisational injustice'

I have a theory that organisations unwittingly create conditions that results in a feeling of injustice – I call this theory 'organisational injustice'.

Organisational injustice is the tendency of organisations to give more work to hard working people and less work to lazy people, resulting in a perceived punishment for being hard working and a perceived endorsement for being lazy.

I became aware of it in the 1980s and have become more convinced over the years of working in the public sector. Let me explain. There is often a built-in systemic dis-incentive to working hard. There is also a systemic incentive to being lazy.

Imagine PC Simon is a hard working, active policeman. Being hard working creates problems for him. More effort brings more arrests. That brings more paper work, which brings more late files. More late files bring more reprimands from the inspector.

More arrests mean more complaints (because people who are arrested often do not like it). More complaints bring more reprimands from the inspector.

More arrests mean more court appearances, which means more disrupted shift patterns. So can you see that working hard can create more problems for PC Simon as feedback?

Continuing the police example, imagine PC Rhodes. He is lazy. He avoids answering the radio. He keeps his head down. He does not investigate suspicious circumstances. If he does not answer the radio and evades work opportunities, the result seems to be positive. Good things happen.

Less effort means reporting fewer offences. That means mean fewer written reports. You have less paper work, so fewer late files. Fewer late files means fewer reprimands from the inspector.

If you don't investigate people, you'll make fewer arrests, which means fewer complaints, which means fewer reprimands from your inspector. Fewer arrests mean fewer court appearances, so that means no appearances at court – an easier life.

Remember that PC Rhodes earns the same money as PC Simon.

Can you see that being lazy creates fewer problems and seems to make good sense to PC Rhodes? Being hard working causes PC Simon problems. Becoming lazy seems to be the solution!

So sometimes, there can be an incentive to do less, and a disincentive to do more.

I have seen that this effect is true in many organisations, not just the police. I have seen the same thing in education, social services and the health service.

Does this effect happen in your place of work?

Are hard working people 'penalised' by being given extra work for no extra reward?

This effect tends to cause poor relationship and atmosphere between the managers/coach and the people being managed. The managers need to inspire good relationships and encourage hard work. They have to do that in spite of the fact that the work-systems seems to punish hard work, and encourage inactivity.

The main way for managers to encourage action cannot always be through cash incentives (you could not pay police bonuses for arresting more people!). The way forward is through praise and appreciation.

Let me give you a concrete example. From 1981 to 1991, I was a Police officer. One evening in 1987, I was starting my night shift at Cheltenham police station (10.00pm until 06.00 am) when, as usual, I checked my in-tray for paper work and information.

There, in my tray I found a slip of paper with a hand written message.

It read 'TO PC 181 FARMER. EXCELLENT ARREST LAST NIGHT! WELL DONE, KEEP UP THE GOOD WORK. CHIEF INSPECTOR DADGE.'

I was amazed. I was used to getting reprimands. This was different. This was positive feedback. I was so pleased !

I showed everyone my note. I was so proud. I had a note from Chief Inspector Dadge!

That note was enough to motivate me for two weeks. And I am still talking about it twenty years later (sad, but true).

Written praise – it is so rare and yet so effective. I do not know how long it took CI Dadge to scribble out that brief note and place it in the internal post. Not long. But its effect was immediate and long lasting. It was a good use of his time, wasn't it?

What surprises me is that it is so unusual for people to give the right amount of praise and positive feedback. As a result, motivation is down, output is down and relationships are not as strong as they could be.

So commit today to be the person who always gives people positive praise and feedback.

Remember:

Organisational injustice must be compensated for. Positive feedback is one way to do it.

A lack of appreciation is an enormous de-motivator

Failing to give positive, on-target feedback is not merely a wasted opportunity to make progress. It is worse than that, it is counter-productive. It is one cause of de-motivation.

You must seize opportunities for praise or you will find people actually working against you, and relationship will suffer.

How to give positive feedback

Four principles for top quality positive feedback:

1 Be specific
   2 Do it soon
      3 Link the action to character and self-image
         4 Ask for more of the same

1 Tell them specifically what it is they have got right

Again, clarity is better that vagueness. Be specific in your positive feedback message. Tell them exactly and precisely what it is that was good. If praise is specific it has two positive consequences.

1   It seems more genuine.

2   It 're-enforces' a specific action, one that you want repeated.

If praise is too generalised, it can have two negative consequences:

1   It can seem insincere
2   It does not encourage any particular behaviour.

Let me give you some examples of each:

Good specific praise might sound like this:

'Jayne, that minutes report you wrote had every single item in the meeting recorded, and you noted all the actions and decisions. That is exactly what I wanted. Well done.'

Whereas vague, not-so-good feedback, might sound like this:

'Jayne, those minutes you wrote for the meeting were super. Well done.'

Both sets of feedback will have a positive effect to some degree, but can you see that the first is better than the second?

The first is better because Jayne knows exactly what it was about her minute writing that the manager thinks is 'super'. Consequently, Jayne feels that the feedback has more meaning, (in terms of sincerity) and knows exactly what to emphasise again in the next set of minutes she writes.

Do it now. Do not wait.

We mentioned this when we were discussing off-target feedback. Let us brush up on the point briefly:

- Give your positive feedback as soon as you can after the event.
- Human brains need feedback in order to learn. And for effective learning the feedback needs to be immediately after the action that caused it.
- If there is no delay between the action and the feedback, learning is enhanced.
- If there is a delay between the action and the feedback, learning is hampered.

Let me give you an example – drinking alcohol. What are the immediate feedback consequences associated to having an alcoholic drink? A nice taste and a warm feeling. What are the delayed consequences, the ones you get the next morning?

A sore head, bad mood and bags under the eyes.

The immediate feedback consequences of alcohol consumption are pleasurable. The delayed consequences are painful. It is the immediate pleasurable consequences that keep people tied to alcohol.

Imagine we reversed 'feedback timings' – the moment you took a sip of wine, you got an intense banging headache, your eyes went baggy and your money vanished? What would happen to wine sales?

Psychologists say that our environment conditions us via consequences. We are conditioned by the immediate consequences of our current actions.

We learn and repeat those actions that result in immediate sensations of pleasure. And we will do this even if, in fact, the actions are destructive (for example, consuming cigarettes, alcohol, and drugs, etc).

We learn and avoid those actions that result in immediate feelings of pain or discomfort. And we will do this even if, in fact, the actions are constructive and beneficial (for example, exercise, studying, consuming cod liver oil, etc).

So, give your positive feedback 'immediately', if you can. The sooner after the event you deliver the feedback message, the more natural and easy the learning will be.

The longer you wait, the more you are working against this principle of human nature.

Make a link from the behaviour to self-image

As a coach, building up self-esteem is part of your role. We noted earlier that positive feedback tends to build self-image.

We can assist the process by linking, in language, the action to the character of the person. Name the positive action, and make a link to the person's personal character, in terms of their self-image.

Do this, and you will make it easy for people to feel good about themselves. So we might extend our earlier example to this:

'Jayne, that minutes report you wrote had every item in the meeting recorded, and you noted all the actions and decisions. You did a really professional job. Well done'

This time we added the concept of Jayne being a 'professional'. We purposefully linked 'professional' to Jayne's self-image, based upon her minute writing skills.

Now, can you see that 'professional' is the kind of comment on her character and self-image that will boost Jayne's self-esteem as a worker? If Jayne accepts herself as a 'professional' that will impact on every aspect of her work, not just minute writing.

You know that people tend to act in accordance with their own self-image. So, to be consistent with her improved self-image, Jayne will hold herself to a higher standard in every aspect of her activity.

This improved self-image will cause her to take superior actions, which will create superior results – which in turn will allow you to come back with more affirming, positive comments.

All this makes for a self-perpetuating positive cycle – which is what we want.

Ask for more of the same

The final step in giving positive feedback that you might want to consider is to 'ask for more of the same'.

I mentioned earlier that we tend to repeat those activities that caused us to receive immediate positive feedback. To a degree that process is automatic and natural and will occur anyway. But why not speed things up and work with the principle, by asking openly for a repetition of the action?

This step is a good idea because you are working in harmony with a natural law of human nature, and improving upon it by reinforcing the tendency with an explicit request.

By asking for more of the same, you are again raising the chances of success, because the person is more likely to remember and repeat the action the next time.

So to sum up, the steps for giving positive feedback are:

- Be specific.
  - Do it soon.
    - Link the action to the character and self-image.
      - Ask for more of the same.

If we now include 'Do it soon' and the request for 'more of the same', our final version of Jayne's minute writing feedback might sound like this:

'Jayne, those minutes reports you gave me this morning were great. You had every item in the meeting recorded, and you noted all the actions and decisions. You did a really professional job. Would you do them like that next time, too? Thanks.'

Learn and use these principles and you will be amazed at the results.

Step 5 – Change in the light of off-target feedback

When a person is given off-target feedback, what should he do with it?

The first task is to analyse it and make a judgement.

The judgement breaks down into these steps:

- Is the feedback true and accurate?
- What does it mean?
- What should I do?

Is the feedback true and accurate?

When you are coaching others, strive to have them be receptive to feedback. However, nobody should accept it blindly, but rather be in a thoughtful frame of mind.

Whenever the person receives critical feedback, the first question is 'is the feedback accurate and true?' Does the feedback represent an accurate statement of the situation or not?

If the trainee, after consideration, decides that the feedback is invalid, he has the right to either reject the feedback or question it.

If he rejects the feedback, he should continue acting in accordance to what he thinks is the correct approach, irrespective of the coach's feedback. In the case of a conflict, reality will be the final arbiter. If the coach was right, the trainee will find his repeated actions are ineffective.

If the trainee is right, the trainee's actions will work, in spite of the doubt inferred by the coach. If the trainee decides that the feedback is invalid, he may challenge the feedback. In other words, he may critique the criticism. The coach is not omnipotent. The feedback may itself be faulty. Do not be upset if your trainee questions your feedback message.

Take this as a compliment. The trainee is thinking about and evaluating your feedback. He has the right to ignore or challenge it. Discuss the feedback and give the reasons and explanation for it. Then let the trainee learn the lesson.

What does it mean?

Let us assume that the trainee has accepted the feedback is accurate and true. The next question is 'What does it mean?'

It means that the trainee's current actions are not likely to produce the result needed. Therefore he will have to change.

What should change?

The 'success formula' says, 'Change in the light of off-target feedback'. This means change one of the following things:

1. Change the goal.
2. Change the plan/ action.

Change the goal

Once the feedback is accepted, it may give enough information to make it clear that the initial goal was inappropriate. The initial purpose was a poor decision and should be abandoned.

An example – one of my clients, Malcolm, recently set up a company. He called it 'Eureka'. His intention was to produce an infra-red light-emitting facemask. The intention was to shine low intensity light onto the face of the wearer. The reason was that infra-red light has positive therapeutic effects on the skin and lessens wrinkles.

The idea was to shine the light onto the skin around the eye and reduce aging. Obviously, Malcolm thought that the theory was good and that he could make money from the venture.

Malcolm is not technical. He did not know enough about the technical nature of infra-red light, so he hired an expert in electronic design to help him with the details. The expert was a Chinese gentleman called Nei. He listened to Malcolm's explanation of his product idea. After a few days of discussion and thought, Nei told Malcolm that the wavelength of light that he intended to use had these qualities.

- They came under the legal definition of LASER. And that took the product into difficult health and safety territory.
- The infra-red frequency was potentially damaging to the retina in the eye.
- Infra-red light is invisible, and the user would be unaware if the light was shining into the eye.
- Initial design and prototype development costs could be up to £100,000.

As a result of Nei's feedback, Malcolm re-evaluated his situation and decided that the goal itself needed to be changed! It was not right for him to continue. He dropped the infra-red light facemask goal and set to work formulating another idea that would serve as a new purpose.

 Sometimes, it is right to abandon a goal.

Change the plan/action
Much more frequently, the 'off-target' feedback should not be taken as a signal to abandon the goal. Rather it is information that indicates that a new plan or improved action is needed.

That means as a coach, you should be encouraging the trainee to think through critical feedback and to use it to devise new improved actions and plans.

Often the result of receiving critical feedback is that the person feels a little disheartened and de-motivated. This is the point where 'The Creed of a Coach' comes into play. You remember the creed of a coach?

**'I no longer see feedback as failure, but only as information
I need to make the next improvement.'**

Your task will be to simultaneously:

1. deliver the off-target feedback
2. encourage the person to evaluate its meaning
3. decided the proper response
4. keep their spirits high as they go through the pain of intellectual growth.

This is a skilled job!

Managing their change
'Change' is inevitable. It is even desirable.

The current situation is unstable and it will change. It is in the process of changing right now. If he wants to keep up, your trainee must be ready to change too. If he is to achieve his goals and win happiness, he must be willing and able to develop and change.

The success formula has change built into it. So to be successful, we must embrace change.

The trouble is of course, that for most people, change is seen as a negative phenomenon. Stability and sameness is seen as good. Certainty is seen as preferable.

As a consequence, asking people to:

- change their habits
  - change their procedures
    - change their thinking
      - change changing methods

… is a difficult and sensitive task. It is your task as the coach.

A quick review of coaching using the success formula

Let us summarise the steps for using the **success formula** as a coaching tool:

The success formula has only five major elements:

1 **Know the outcome.**
2 **Formulate a plan.**
3 **Take action.**
4 **Gather the feedback.**
5 **Change in the light of off-target feedback.**

In respect of the person you are training or coaching, the success formula translates into the following process:

1 Demonstrate, role model, describe or show the person the desired outcome.

2 Break the task down into a logical sequence of smaller steps and have the person understand the structure of the task.

3 Have them take action. Let them have a go.

4 Provide the person with both on-target encouraging feedback and off-target corrective feedback. (Review the notes on feedback.)

5 Help the person to change and improve his actions in response to the critical, off-target feedback he is receiving. Keep him from

imagining the off-target feedback represents failure. Many people do feel that critical feedback means 'they can't do it'. Your role, as the coach is to prevent that thought from taking root.

6   Return to step one.

Full circle

So now we have come full circle, as our discussion of change as part of the success formula has bought us back to the topic we started with, improvement through change.

Turn to the front of the book and review the first chapter on change. Reconsider the issue of 'baby steps change' and 'revolutionary change', this time in the context of training and coaching others.

The success formula is cyclical, so it is natural for me to ask you to go around and start this material again. As you repeat the material, your focus will be drawn to different elements.

Take the time to re read the ideas and practice the techniques.

You will benefit yourself and others if you do.

Thank you.

The Corporate Coach

The corporate coach is a training company whose purpose is to present a theory of effective action for organisational managers and leaders together with skills to put the theory into practice.

In essence, our desire is to help you define your goals and standards and then to achieve them.

We have a number of expert trainers who will tailor the principles to your context.

Chris Farmer is the leader of the corporate coach training company, which he started in 1997.

"I started the company because I believe there are many people who are searching for practical advice on how to get the most out of themselves and other people.

Now more than ever organisations need their people to be productive and happy. That means that the leadership and management of people cannot be left to arbitrary feelings or whim. Rather, leadership and management should be a system of professional skills that employs definite, named principles. Our goal is to set out these principles and discuss how to implement them in practice."

Corporate Coach Group, 6 Broadway Close,
Prestbury, Cheltenham, Glos GL52 3EA
Telephone: 01242 254706
E-mail: info@corporatecoachgroup.co.uk

Methods

One-to-one coaching

Individual coaching may be the best form of learning for certain people.

That way, a person can be totally free to address any issue that may be affecting performance, without fear that others are judging.

Groups

We most frequently work with groups of between 8 and 20 delegates.

We present ideas and practice technique. It is a good opportunity to clarify thinking by conversation with others. We like this approach.

Telephone coaching

This is similar to 'one-to-one coaching' but is done on the phone.

This can be useful because sometimes people need to discuss issues with a person who is not directly associated with the team.

CD audio

Repetition helps recall. So we produce a number of audio CDs that focus on key issues of leadership and management.

That way, your team can fully integrate the best ideas into their daily action.

We are extremely happy with your training message and style. That's why we keep using you. We always get excellent comments back from the delegates so we are happy to recommend you to others.

Peter Bowler
Renishaw plc

We always get good feedback from your programmes. People come back to us and say that they have learned things they can actually use.

Tracy Beaver
Worcestershire Council

CONTACT

Corporate Coach Group, 6 Broadway Close
Prestbury, Cheltenham,
Gloucestershire, GL52 3EA

telephone: 01242 254706
Fax: 01242 254706
Email: info@corporatecoachgroup.co.uk
Website: www.corporatecoachgroup.co.uk